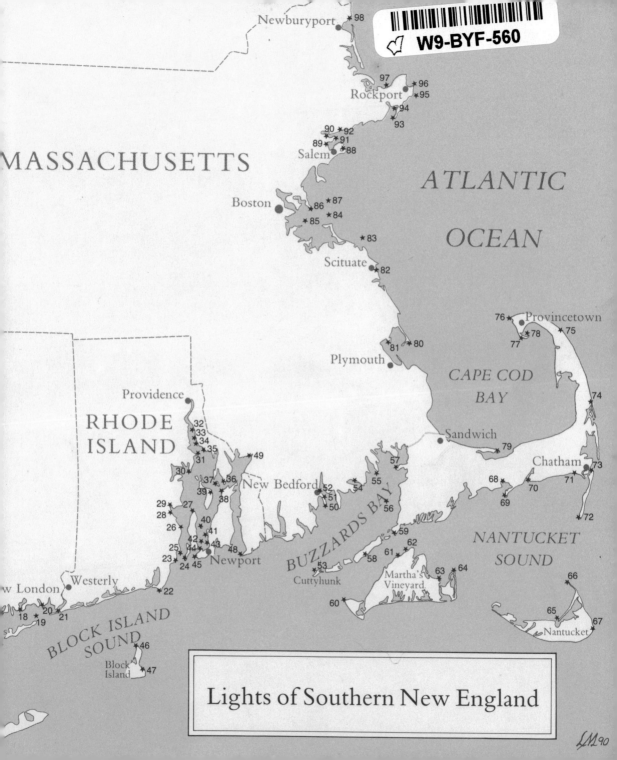

MASSACHUSETTS

ATLANTIC

OCEAN

Newburyport ★ 98

W9-BYF-560

★ 97   ★ 96
Rockport   ★ 95
        ★ 94
        ★ 93

90 ★ ★ 92
89 ★ ★ 91
Salem ★ 88

Boston   86 ★ ★ 87
        ★ 84
    85 ★

    ★ 83

Scituate   ★ 82

        76 ★   Provincetown
            ★ 78   ★ 75
        77

        81 ★ ★ 80

Plymouth   CAPE COD
        BAY

            ★ 74

Providence   Sandwich   79
        ★   ★
RHODE
ISLAND   Chatham ★ 73
    32   68   70 ★ 71
    33   ★   ★ 69
    34   57
    35 49   ★   72
    31   55
    30   36   54   56   NANTUCKET
    37   52   SOUND
    39   38   51
        50
    29 27
    28   59
    26   40   62   66
        41   61   65
    25 42 44 43 48   58   63 64   67
    23 24 45   Newport   53   Martha's   Nantucket
    22   Cuttyhunk   Vineyard
New London Westerly   60

18 20 21
19
BLOCK ISLAND
SOUND

        ★ 46
Block
Island   ★ 47

Lights of Southern New England

ℒℳ90

KINDLY LIGHTS

Best wishes,

Sarah Gleason

KINDLY LIGHTS

A History of the Lighthouses of Southern New England

SARAH C. GLEASON

With a Foreword by John Casey

BEACON PRESS • BOSTON

Beacon Press
25 Beacon Street
Boston, Massachusetts 02108-2800

Beacon Press books
are published under the auspices of
the Unitarian Universalist Association of Congregations.

98 97 96 95 94 93 92 91   8 7 6 5 4 3 2 1

Text design by Christine Leonard Raquepaw

Library of Congress Cataloging-in-Publication Data

Gleason, Sarah C.
    Kindly lights : a history of the lighthouses of southern New England / Sarah C.
Gleason.
        p.   cm.
    Includes bibliographical references.
    ISBN 0-8070-5107-1
    1. Lighthouses—New England—History.   I. Title.
VK1024.N38G54   1991
387.1′55—dc20   90-52591
                                                                        CIP

With love and appreciation

I dedicate this book to my mother,

Elizabeth Wilson Fischer,

and to my husband,

Tom Gleason,

without whose care and support

I would not have written

Kindly Lights.

Lead, kindly Light, amid the encircling gloom;

Lead thou me on!

The night is dark, and I am far from home,

Lead thou me on!

Keep thou my feet, I do not ask to see

The distant scene; one step enough for me.

John Henry Newman

(1801–90)

Contents

List of Illustrations

Text Illustrations

Catalog Illustrations

Foreword

I have three reasons for liking this book, and I think all three will hold for most readers.

There is of course romance. Lighthouses are as romantic as castles. They are symbols of noble solitude. Living in a tower on a sea-sprayed rock you could be Andromeda, Rapunzel; you could have thoughts like Byron's, Tennyson's or Jean-Jacques Rousseau's. They are stations of duty—the foghorn or bell, the sweeping beam of light are desperate messages in the nick of time. I wanted to read *Kindly Lights*, having found in middle age that discovering more about objects of romance is preferable to not knowing; either the romance is dispelled or it is deepened and prolonged.

Stephen Jones's *Harbor of Refuge* is another lighthouse book, quite different in scope and structure. It is about Jones's year as a Coast Guard lighthouse keeper. It is a witty and reflective memoir, and full of sobering detail. Jones makes clear that perched on top of his tower on a small rock quite far from land, he was sometimes bored, sometimes driven a little dingo by his mates, and, during a monumental storm, justifiably terrified of being toppled into the sea. (See Chapter 6 of this book for several accounts of lighthouses being engulfed.) But Jones was saddened when his lighthouse was automated; his eyes were wide open but a version of the romance stayed intact. Broader in scope, *Kindly Lights* replaces some notions about lighthouses, but strengthens their spell.

The second reason for my liking this book arises from my own experience, but it can easily be adopted and enlarged on by readers who have spent time in the dark on salt water, especially by those who have ever wondered where they were. I lived on a very small island for four years. I thought I knew about boats when I moved there. I even said to someone that I thought it would be no different from living on the mainland, I'd just be using a boat instead of a car. It didn't take long for me to wise up. I never got really good at the skills I could have used, but I got over that initial jauntiness. I'm grateful that I didn't end up hurting anyone during my raw period. I'm also grateful for the things people taught me and for the things I picked up on my own.

There was no phone or power line to the island, no police or fire service. I came to rely on a lot of nineteenth-century technology, especially since the two boat motors we had didn't work regularly. Rowing to town and back in the dark, sometimes in fog, I was able to imagine some of the difficulties of an earlier life in boats, although my experiences were very small-scale. From time to time I got lost—or at least momentarily misplaced. I got to know the Wickford light and the top lights of the Jamestown Bridge, a glimpse of which in a low-lying fog could clear up the major question. There was also a useful light in the huge north window of the converted barn where my parents-in-law lived. At night they drew scarlet curtains across the window which produced a glowing scarlet block of light in a light fog. Rowing back to the island from their house I could keep a clear course straight home with the scarlet dot receding over the port quarter—so long as they didn't turn out the lights. I was pleased to learn in Ms. Gleason's work that a precursor of the lighthouse on Nantucket was a lamp in the window when a boat or ship was expected.

On the island we couldn't keep a light burning all night. We had a generator, but we only ran it for an hour or so in the evening to power the water pump and the CB radio. Several times in the course of four years power yachts coming up the bay hit the island, or one of the many rocks around it. One fellow was mad as hell and thought I should have showed a light. That particular night there was enough moonlight to have made out the island, but his wheelhouse was too lit up for him to see much of the darker real world.

All these little experiences nudged me towards one point as I tried to imagine American life before 1900. It was a lot darker.

I spent a month during my island years at the Outward Bound School on Hurricane Island, about a dozen miles off the Maine coast. I noticed that one of the first shocks to a lot of people from cities was that they had never been in so much dark. A little dark, a momentary dark, a closet or a basement. But not this vast darkness! Darkness farther than they could see by day, farther than they could hear, farther than they could have walked if they weren't on an island.

It was on a coast even more vastly dark than today's that the first American lighthouses were built. As I read Ms. Gleason's history, the incidents and anecdotes she has set out provoked my own memories of dark and light, and tucked them neatly in to her ordered chronicle.

An amateur interest in history is my third reason for falling for *Kindly Lights*. The book concerns itself with lighthouses, highly specialized structures of which there were only a handful in New England during the eighteenth century, and even in the nineteenth there were fewer lighthouses than there were cities. Yet this history of a navigational specialty in one small part of America calls up some of the great historical issues of American life: the problem of a communal enterprise in a nation increasingly devoted to individualism, both for the spirit of it and for the profit. Early on, the seafaring community had to consider the advantages and disadvantages of local control versus federal control. And as a lighthouse system developed in the nineteenth century there was more and more tension between a letting-things-be policy (which had the advantages of set training and settled knowledge of what kind of signals marked which channels and shoals) and incorporating new technology. And of course there was the problem of contractors coming to feed in the always fertile intertidal zone where federal expenditure for a public benefit overlaps with private entrepreneurship. Ms. Gleason's treatment of this last issue is occasionally a cautionary tale of venality and bungling, but it is also satisfying that, on the whole, enough good people turned up with inventions, organizing ability, reforming zeal, and, at the operational level, the devotion to duty necessary to keep the lights lit.

All these issues are recurring ones, and there is an interesting perspective to be gained from seeing these various American dilemmas played out through the lighthouse system. There is a comical passage in the book about the back-and-forth hiring and firing of two Gay Head lighthouse keepers under the spoils system. They were Tweedledum and Tweedledee except that one was a Democrat and the other a Whig.

Ms. Gleason gives a good example in miniature of the increasing rapacious bustle of the nineteenth century in the tale she tells of Winslow Lewis. He ended up being both the inspector of lighthouses and a not-surprisingly successful bidder on contracts for construction and repair, the specifications for which he devised. He also had contracts for supplying the lights with whale oil. His maneuverings against David Melville, who was a pioneer in gas light, are a foreshadowing of the robber-baron mode of operation. The reformers of the lighthouse system triumphed in 1852, partly through energy and good sense, but also through the lucky circumstance that some members of Congress were on board a ship that was held up by a light going out.

The *plus-ça-change* perspective of recurring themes is only part of Ms. Gleason's history. She also gives a good sense of how different we have become, of how the particular matter of our lives has changed. The illustrations she has chosen for this volume are a correlative of this quality of her narrative. The picture of Crowninshield wharf in Salem is a reminder of how crucial a little cluster of sailing ships was to our commerce—of how small a toehold we had on the continent. Her description of the early technical efforts and failures of the lighthouses is interesting in itself— and the apparatuses (the parabolic reflector, the Argand lamp, the Fresnel lens) are fascinating—but they also provide by implication a sense of how feeble we were technically, how far we were from Europe (where these things were already in use), how long it took information to travel and for devices to be adopted and put in place. We get a sense too of how isolated one part of America was from another and of how so many ordinary people lived in a way that we today would think of as camping out.

This is a story of a time when setting out a light was simultaneously much more difficult and more crucial. Nowadays commercial vessels have LORAN (Long-Range Navigation) a network of radio beams that fix a ship's position anywhere at sea with a margin of error the size of a football field. Ships also have radar and sonar with which they can "see" other vessels, the coast, the sea bottom and buoys tipped with radar reflectors. All of these devices have come into general use since my childhood. Until well into this century, mariners depended more on their direct senses. They could figure out where they were by celestial navigation or by dead reckoning, but *at best* there was a margin of error of close to a mile. Given the unpredictable speed of a sailing voyage, the chances of making landfall by day and in clear weather weren't very good. Finding the safe channel into port depended on direct perception. You might hear surf, you might smell land, you might drop a leadline and feel the bottom, but best of all would be to see. A good way to read this book about lighthouses is to contemplate how the coast appeared from the sea, how it must have felt to be looking for a channel a good deal smaller than the uncertainty of your position, to be sailing in the dark and then to see the light.

John Casey

Preface

There be three things which are too wonderful for
me . . . the way of an eagle in the air; the way of a serpent
upon a rock; the way of a ship in the midst of the sea. . . .

—Proverbs 30:18, 19

Our conquest of the sea indeed *is* wondrous. But today, when even outer space is not too far to journey, we can easily forget where we have come from. Lighthouses are reminders for some of us of a simpler, slower time that was not so very long ago. When much else is changing so rapidly, these spare, functional towers have the power to make us pause and reflect on what has been.

Technologically, lighthouses represent a late stage in development of aids to navigation, those varied means by which mariners are guided in their voyages. Once, the only source of help was other sailors, passing on to one another their knowledge of coastlines, currents, and other hazards. At first, such information was conveyed by word of mouth, and later in print. Charts were drawn up to indicate natural landmarks and manmade seamarks. Sailing directions, too, were printed and disseminated. At ports of call, men erected beacons as markers and sometimes also lit fires for the guidance of ships at night. Lighthouses came later, a final step in a navigational science of providing guidance through visual means.

Highly sophisticated technological systems are now replacing lighthouses. From the vantage of earth-encircling satellites beaming their signals to mariners, these life-saving towers are inconsequential specks on the face of the globe. Many today are useless, reminders of paths of commerce that have come and gone. Lighthouses that still shine beacons do so automatically, without the keepers who cared for them and watched for those at sea.

As the world represented by lighthouses slips away, attitudes toward these structures have been changing. Once little noticed except by navigators, lighthouses today symbolize a romantically remembered past. Many individuals and groups have become active in their preservation, and new uses are being found for lights no longer active. Fragments of the past are being preserved in many lighthouse museums.

This book grew from such an effort to preserve the memory of Rhode Island's lighthouses and their keepers. The first steps, funded by the Rhode Island Committee for the Humanities, were a traveling exhibit sponsored by the Rhode Island Department of Environmental Management and a National Register Thematic Nomination submitted by the Rhode Island Historical Preservation Commission. Eventually, the exhibit found a permanent home in the Beavertail Lighthouse Museum, developed by the Rhode Island Parks Association.

As director of this exhibit, "The Light Must Be Kept Burning," I discovered historic material suggesting a much richer story than I had anticipated. Particularly for the more obscure period preceding the lighthouse reforms of 1852, the record was fragmented and yet enticing. Eventually, working in the library of the Newport Historical Society, I came across a handwritten "Meteorological Diary" by David Melville, recording a remarkable experiment in gas lighting at Beavertail Lighthouse in 1817 and 1818. Though Melville succeeded in producing a cleaner, brighter light and with less difficulty than that produced by the whale oil lamps in general use, the government did not renew his contract. Melville charged subterfuge by Nantucket whalers fearful of losing control of the lights. When I learned that this claim was supported by the reputable William Ellery, signer of the Declaration of Independence, I suspected that I might have the beginning of a book.

This brief history of the early American lighthouse administration, viewed through lighthouses of southern New England, is the result. Though of course lighthouses were built up and down the coast, they long predominated in this most populous region. The first four lighthouses were established in Massachusetts, Rhode Island, and Connecticut, and here is where the struggle for control of navigational aids was played out most intensely. Geographically and economically, the area was more closely bound than Maine and New Hampshire. The lighthouses of northern New England, so affected by inhospitable climate and jagged coastline, deserve a story of their own.

I have concentrated on lighthouses to the exclusion of lightships, buoys, beacons, fog signals, and other aids of importance to navigation for a number of reasons. I have not tried to write a comprehensive history but rather have focused on economic and political influences that shaped lighthouse administration. Lightships, totaling around thirty by 1852, were notable for their inadequacy in marking treacherous offshore points; their introduction after 1820 did not affect the story of overall administration. The history of lightships is certainly worth telling—one sailor described his term on board one as similar to "solitary confinement combined with the horrors of sea-sickness"—and would no doubt illuminate aspects of the larger picture.*

The story that follows begins with early attempts at navigational safety leading to establishment of the first lighthouses in North America. Once the federal government established responsibility for the country's navigational aids, its fumbling efforts made management of the lights vulnerable to the influence of contractors such as Winslow Lewis. David Melville's experiments with gas lighting and his later conflicts with Lewis shed light on "big business" at the time. The history of this period concludes, in Chapter 5, with the struggle to reform lighthouse administration, culminating in the establishment of the U.S. Lighthouse Board.

Lighthouse keeping is the subject of Chapter 6. Until the present day, keepers, the men and women on the front lines, have been the ones to make or break a lighthouse system, but how well they have functioned was linked closely with the character of the administration of which they are a part. This final chapter offers an overview of the history of lighthouse keeping in the United States and concludes with the personal accounts of some twentieth-century lighthouse keepers and family members. In 1989, completion of the Coast Guard's Lighthouse Automation and Modernization Program ended lighthouse keeping in the United States as practiced for almost three centuries (with the exception of Boston Light, which by special act of Congress in 1989 is to remain permanently manned, to preserve its special historic character.) This chapter ends with the stories of some of those who lived in the lighthouses of southern New England, stories collected first from interviews conducted for the Rhode Island Lighthouse Project and later from those who had lived in lighthouses elsewhere. These reminiscences remind us of a close bond of affection between people and structure that will not exist again.

---

*David Stick, *North Carolina Lighthouses* (Raleigh: North Carolina Department of Cultural Resources, 1984), p. 28.

Acknowledgments

Many have helped me in my pursuit of this fascinating subject, including those who have worked for the Light House Service or the Coast Guard, those who are working to preserve endangered lighthouses, and those who simply love lighthouses for reasons of their own. I here offer my thanks and gratitude to many who have shared with me their time and knowledge: Dr. Gerald Abbott, Virginia Adams, the late Luella Ball, Carole Bell, Ken Black, Richard Boonisar, Larry Bradner, Edmont Clark, Terry Cramer, Don Davidson, Hadassah Davis, Elinor de Wire, Bob Downey, Raymond Goddard, Roger Gustafson, Philip Haring, John Herzen, Sheila Hogg, Jay Hyland, Alda Kaye, Sallie Latimer, Bert Lippincott, Ken Morse, Jean Napier, George Nemetz, Anne M. Preuss, Arthur Railton, Dr. Robert Scheina, William Sherman, Charles Silverman, Dan Snydacker, Dorothy Templeton, Dick Thompson, Donald Treworgy, Wally Welch, Bill Worthington, Wick York, and the many keepers and family members who have shared their stories with me. For their special interest and support, I am especially indebted to Lisa Pachter and Wayne Wheeler, and, of course, to Tom Gleason.

KINDLY LIGHTS

1

Bonfires, Beacons, and Colonial Lighthouses

Our seafaring people are brave, despise danger, and reject
such precautions of safety, being cowards only in one sense,
that of *fearing* to be *thought afraid*."

—BENJAMIN FRANKLIN, "Maritime Observations"

The purpose of a lighthouse is to tell mariners where they are at night. If the coast is familiar, the beacon will be a reassuring sign. For sailors unsure of where they are, a lighthouse will warn their craft away from danger. The history of lighthouse technology is the story of making this life-saving function ever more efficient.

Bonfires were the earliest signals for guiding boats at night, and the first lighthouses were little more than fires of coal or wood set atop an open tower. Early lighthouses consumed huge amounts of fuel—one on Scotland's Isle of May burned a ton of coal on a single windy night—and their unfocused light was quickly diffused. Sailors close enough to see the fire might be too close to change course. Worse yet, one bonfire looked much like another, so such signals were of limited use to mariners unsure of their bearings.[1]

Toward the end of the eighteenth century, a sharp increase in commerce created demand for more and better lighthouses. Poorly marked coasts saw the wreck of many a vessel that had journeyed safely across the ocean. Approximately one vessel a day was lost to shipwreck in 1800, according to a reputable insurer.[2] Fortunately, the same technology that fueled the growth of manufacture and trade held the promise of better lighting. When glass became available, the previously open lantern

Fig. 1. Dugeness Lighthouse on the southern coast of England, illuminated with fire in open lantern room. From a receipt for lighthouse dues dated 19 December 1690.

rooms in lighthouses, for instance, could be furnished with candles or lamps rather than with coal or wood. Though dimmer than bonfires, these substitutes became brighter when backed with reflectors. As early as 1669, a flat mirror was used at the Landsort Lighthouse in Sweden. By the eighteenth century, experimenters were learning what form of reflector worked best.

The usefulness of a reflector stems from the fact that the angle of a ray of light falling on a surface (the incident ray) is equal to that of the ray leaving the reflector (the reflected ray). It was soon learned that, with a flat reflecting surface, the ray merely returns in the direction from which it came, with diminished strength, while rays reflecting from a concave surface converge and intensify. If the reflector is spherical, most of the rays are merely directed back toward the light source. A parabolic surface, however, reflects rays back toward the viewer in a beam of concentrated light equal to the diameter of the reflector.[3] This property of the parabolic reflector made it vital in improving lighthouse technology.

The first parabolic reflector for navigational purposes may have been devised by Liverpool dockmaster William Hutchinson in 1763. By the end of the century, at

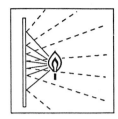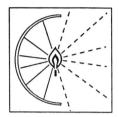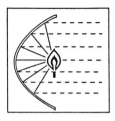

Fig. 2. A parabola is the most suitable shape for a lighthouse reflector because it intensifies the rays by projecting them in a cone of light. A flat surface merely projects the rays back in the direction from which they came. A spherical shape reflects the rays toward each other. Drawn by Wendy Andrews.

least eleven lighthouses on the south and southeast coasts of England were equipped with parabolic reflectors.[4]

Even more important in the history of lighting was the Argand lamp, developed by Swiss chemist Aimé Argand around 1782. The principal feature of this lamp was a new kind of wick, hollow in the middle so that air could pass through its center. The greater combustion that resulted produced a cleaner, brighter flame than the older solid wicks. With improvements that followed, such as a curved glass chimney that created a draft and so steadied the flame, an Argand lamp could produce a light as bright as eight candles.

Lighthouses have always been expensive to build and maintain, and responsibility for them has varied over time. In the Middle Ages, when commerce and defense were closely linked, light towers served as fortifications as well as navigational aids. Merchants and rulers, in the Hanseatic League in northern Europe and in Genoa and Venice in the south, shared an interest in their establishment and cooperated in their upkeep.[5] In England, by contrast, lighthouses were awarded by monarchs to their followers, and the tolls collected were a source of great wealth. Such lights seldom contributed much to the safety of navigation. On the contrary, they were often dim and poorly maintained.

English rulers gradually turned to mariners for help with navigational matters. In the Middle Ages, Trinity House mariners' guilds had been formed in a number of ports. Religious in origin, they also aided mariners in distress or their widows and orphaned children. In 1514, a royal charter made Trinity House of Deptford Strond a pilotage authority, and, in 1566, an act "touching Sea Markes and Maryners" granted it the right to collect fees for building and maintaining certain beacons. The preface to this act stated that many lives had been lost as the coast was developed.

> forasmuch as by destroying and taking away of certain Steeples, Woods and other Markes, standing upon the mayne shores adjoinyng to the Sea Costes of thys Realme of England and Wales, being as Beakons and Markes of auncyent tyme accustomed for seafaring Men to save and keep them and the shippes in their Charge from sundry Daungers thereto incident. . . . have by the lacke of suche Marks of late yeres been myscarried, peryshed and lost in the Sea, to the great Detryment and Hurte of the Common Weale, and the perysheng of no smale number of People.[6]

As time passed, Trinity House played a larger role in sea marking but was slow to establish lighthouses. Perhaps mariners thought that lighthouses were too unreliable to be useful or that they might guide enemies approaching at night. In the course of the seventeenth century, however, as technology improved and coastal defense was strengthened, Trinity House added a dozen lights to those managed privately. These mainly served the coal trade on the east coast of England.

Through much of the eighteenth century, Scottish coasts were marked by only a few private lights, even though sea traffic increased dramatically as trade developed with the American colonies. In 1786, at the request of magistrates of coastal towns, Parliament established the Northern Lighthouse Board to oversee improvements to Scotland's navigational lighting. In Ireland, too, a commission to administer lighthouses was established in the eighteenth century, known then as the Ballast Board.

The new world had been colonized for nearly a century before the first lighthouse was built in North America. To assist with navigation, however, early colonists erected beacons on prominent points of land, and some were even lighted with a wire basket of glowing coals hung from the top. As early as 1763, a beacon marked Allerton Point in Boston's outer harbor, and that city's Beacon Hill and Beacon Island (renamed Brewster's Island by the time the Boston light was built there) also had such seamarks.

One of the earliest lighted beacons was at Beavertail Point opposite the town of Newport. Located at the southern end of Conanicut Island dividing the east and west passages of Narragansett Bay, the point was also a landfall for many vessels arriving from sea. Probably not long after Newport was founded in 1639, bonfires were lit on Beavertail for the guidance of vessels at night. Hostilities in Europe

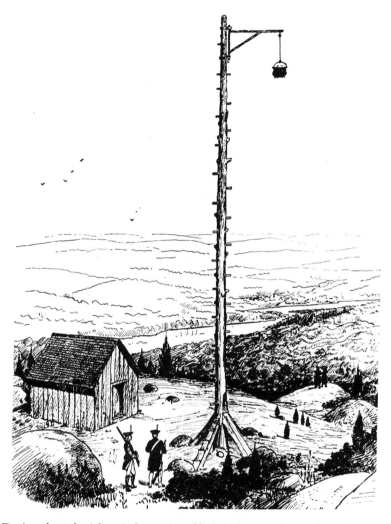

Fig. 3. During the colonial period, a series of lighted beacons beamed warning up the coast of Narragansett Bay at the approach of enemy vessels. Such beacons, lighted with a bucket of burning coal or okum, also served as navigational aids. Courtesy of the Rhode Island Historical Society.

eventually compelled the colonists to build coastal defenses, including a watch house at Beavertail. In 1705, after the onset of Queen Anne's War, the Town Council ordered a chimney—perhaps housing an elevated bonfire—"built upon the Watch-house at Beaver Tail by the Indians belonging to the town."

Connecticut that same year stationed seven men near a beacon on the west end of Fisher's Island, ready to warn the mainland should enemy ships appear.[7] During later hostilities—the French and Indian War and the American Revolution—Rhode Islanders established a chain of beacons up Narragansett Bay ready to warn of approaching enemy vessels.

Elsewhere in southern New England, beacons served the growing Nantucket whale fishery. Whenever a ship was expected at night, Nantucket islanders would display a light from the window of a private dwelling.[8] In addition, islanders supplied oil for beacons elsewhere. One such beacon was at Tarpaulin Cove on Naushon Island. In 1726, its owner, Zaccheus Lumbert, petitioned the Massachusetts General Court, arguing for relief from paying duty on the liquor he served in his tavern nearby because of public benefit provided by his lighthouse, which was kept at his own expense and which he claimed to be "a means of saving many vessels from being lost, & found to be of great advantage to Navigation." The court was not impressed with his arguments, however, and ordered Lumbert to pay six pounds.[9]

As some steps were taken to improve navigational safety, Yankee habits of self-reliance and resistance to change occasionally worked against improvement. In *Accounts of Shipwreck and of Other Disasters at Sea, Designed To Be Interesting and Useful to Mariners, with an Appendix, Containing Dr. Payson's Address to Seamen, and a Few Prayers for Their Use*, the author, a "Friend of Seamen," lamented the needless loss of life at sea. To avert tragedy, he suggested such commonsense steps as hanging a light on deck at night to prevent collision and securing axes to the deck so they would not be lost when most needed, to cut away the masts of a capsized ship. In particular, he repeated a recommendation of Benjamin Franklin's that ships be equipped with swimming anchors to retard the drift of a vessel toward shore if caught in a storm. Of the recent wreck of the *Albion*, the author lamented that, had a swimming anchor been used, "she would not have struck until after daylight, and several valuable lives would have been saved."[10]

Benjamin Franklin's thoughts on navigational safety, written down on his final voyage home from England, were published as "Maritime Observations." In these,

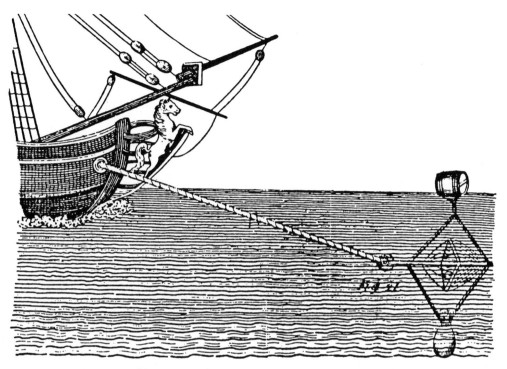

Fig. 4. Benjamin Franklin proposed that swimming anchors such as this one, to retard a ship's drift in a storm, should be standard equipment on all vessels. His advice was largely ignored, however, and for many years ships continued to be wrecked helplessly when caught in a driving wind.

he offered tips on how to minimize strain on an anchor cable (use a pulley), how to prevent being struck by lightning (run a lightning rod up the mast when a storm approached), how to avoid striking another ship in the night (keep a lookout, beat a drum, or ring a bell), and how to prevent leaking ships from sinking. Here he mentioned the "well-known practice of the Chinese, to divide the hold of a great ship into a number of separate chambers, . . . so that, if a leak should spring in one of them, the others are not affected by it." He also proposed two versions of the swimming anchor and noted with satisfaction that Captain Truxtun, the shipmaster with whom he was sailing, had one aboard. (Truxton was in this regard exceptional.)

Fig. 5. This chart was prepared at the request of Benjamin Franklin while serving as colonial postmaster general, to assist British navigators in avoiding the Gulf Stream when crossing the Atlantic. Nantucket shipmasters, familiar with the current, made the trip in a much shorter time. But the British disdained the advice and persisted in their slower ways. Courtesy of the American Antiquarian Society, Philadelphia.

Franklin's suggestions concerning ship construction are particularly startling: "Would it not be a more secure method of planking ships, if, instead of thick single planks laid horizontally, we were to use planks of half the thickness, and lay them double and across each other?" No wonder so many vessels were lost if only a single plank kept out the ocean! The exhortations of the "Friend of Seamen" and of Franklin are surely an indication of unthinking and widespread neglect of ship safety at the time.[11]

On the other hand, the know-how of Yankee captains often proved sounder than the navigational science on which the British relied. Franklin elsewhere told the story of complaints by British shipowners that their packets from Falmouth to New York took two weeks longer than American vessels voyaging from London to Rhode Island. Franklin, then postmaster, investigated why this should be and learned from a Captain Folger of Nantucket that Yankee captains traveling west avoided the Gulf Stream, which the British captains did not:

> We are well acquainted with that stream . . . because in our pursuit of whales, which keep near the sides of it, but are not to be met with in it, we run down along the side, and frequently cross it to change our side; and in crossing it we have sometimes met and spoke with those packets, who were in the middle of it, and stemming it. We have informed them that they were stemming a current, that it was against them to the value of three miles an hour; and advised them to cross it and get out of it; but they were too wise to be counselled by simple American fishermen.

Franklin had Folger mark the Gulf Stream on a chart along with directions for avoiding it when sailing from Europe to America. He had the chart engraved and sent it to Falmouth for use of the packet captains, "who slighted it however."[12] In 1875, the accuracy of Folger's map was confirmed by Alexander Starbuck, who in his famous history of American whaling noted that "this sketch made over a century ago is substantially the same as if found on charts of the present day."[13]

It is known that Yankee shipmasters long continued to navigate by means of dead reckoning rather than with instruments such as those used by British vessels to determine latitude and longitude by measuring the positions of heavenly bodies. In dead reckoning, position is calculated from speed and direction with reference only to the point of departure, with the captain recording his route on a chart each day. In his *Maritime History of Massachusetts*, Samuel Eliot Morison tells the story of an American vessel seized in Denmark in 1810, at a time when that country was at war with England. The Danes charged that absence of chart or sextant proved that the boat must have sailed from the nearby British Isles. American shipmasters in the port, however, protested: "We have frequently made voyages from America without [these] articles and we are fully persuaded that every seaman with common nautical knowledge can do the same."[14]

Colonial seamen began to form associations for mutual aid, similar in this respect to the Trinity House guilds. The first was established in Boston in 1742, followed

Fig. 6. This seal was engraved for the Boston Marine Society in 1754 by Boston silver-smith Nathaniel Hurd. The society had requested a seal "representing a Ship arriving at the light House from a storm and the Sun breaking out of the clouds." Courtesy of the Boston Marine Society.

by the Newport Marine Society a decade later. The Salem Marine Society was incorporated in 1772, and thirty-three years later shipmasters in the China trade formed the Salem East India Marine Society. (The Peabody Museum of Salem was founded by the latter in 1799 as a repository for exotic artifacts gathered abroad.) Portland, Portsmouth, Newburyport, Marblehead, and Providence all formed marine societies, as did ports to the south.[15]

These associations provided insurance for members and their families. Dues and fines were put into a "Box," the society bank, and funds were paid out as needed. Fines were levied for infractions that included quarrelsomeness, profanity, absence from meetings while at home and in good health, and failure to attend the funeral of a member or his wife. The Salem East India Society also fined a member who failed to "communicate in writing his observations of the bearings and distances of all Capes and Head Lands of the Latitudes and Longitude of Islands, rocks and Shoals of sounding tides and Currents of unusual occurances, Storms and accidents with all other observations, which he may judge useful."[16] In the absence of other

Fig. 7. This section of the seal of the Providence Marine Society depicts a rescue of ship-wrecked mariners at Beavertail Lighthouse. From a 1796 engraving by William Hamlin after a painting by Thomas Young. Courtesy of the Rhode Island Historical Society.

forms of insurance, these funds were vitally important. To members "reduced on Shore by Old Age or Sickness" who had paid dues for seven years, the Boston Marine Society gave annual relief payments. To the widow of a deceased member, it paid back all that had been paid in plus whatever else could be afforded at the time.[17]

These societies also functioned as social and professional clubs. Members met regularly, shared information from their voyages, prepared sailing directions, and occasionally petitioned government officials for help with navigational matters such as preparation of charts. Outsiders sometimes called on societies to evaluate charts or nautical inventions. In 1792, the Boston Marine Society commended John Foster Williams, captain of the first U.S. revenue cutter, for his efforts to distill fresh water from salt water and noted that "he also introduced the various kinds of Water thus

Extracted some of which was made into Punch & highly agreeable, as respected taste and smell, being quite pure." A few years later, it criticized a chart of Georges Bank and Nantucket Shoals presented by Edmund March Blunt for lack of proof that the work was based on actual observations.[18]

Preparation of written sailing directions for their home ports was a useful service performed by marine societies. These were published in local gazettes or as single broadsides, collected by navigators along with what charts they could find, and carried always on voyages at sea. Since American vessels could afford few navigational instruments, commonly only a compass for finding direction, a lead line for sounding depth, and a chip log and sand glass for measuring speed, these directions were all the more valuable for unfamiliar coasts. Rocky harbors were treacherous even for those who knew them, as directions for Salem suggest: "The Endeavours Rocks always under water with 4 feet at the lowest ebb, are found by bring[ing] Black Rock in the wake of Cat Island, so as to see the Island on each side & to bring a House on Marblehead between Peach's Point & Nogg's [Naugus] Head in Hollow, over a rock laying at the entrance of that Hollow, & the Endeavours are then within you."[19]

Preparation of charts was beyond the capacity of marine societies, and for many years the best ones of North America were pre-Revolutionary British Admiralty charts. Toward the end of the eighteenth century, American printers began to publish pirated versions of these and other charts. The most enterprising proved to be Edmund March Blunt, who in 1796 issued the first edition of *The American Coast Pilot*. Undaunted by earlier criticism from the Boston Marine Society, in this work he claimed, "as far as possible, to give accurate descriptions of the coasts and harbors of the United States, and directions for approaching and departing from the same; and the rocks and shoals, and the buoys, beacons, and lighthouses, erected to guide the mariner in his perilous course."[20]

The book was an immediate success. Though initially only a collection of existing charts and sailing directions, in 1806 Blunt began adding charts of his own and other original material. Blunt also published Nathaniel Bowditch's *New American Practical Navigator*, first issued in 1802 and still in use today.

In 1791, the Salem Marine Society undertook an ambitious project, the building of a beacon on Baker's Island by private subscription. The previous year, the society had admitted ship owners to its membership for the first time, and perhaps it was they who induced the group to undertake this and other markings of the treacherous harbor. Though Congress had asserted its responsibility for navigational aids two years before, the society no doubt believed that it could act more swiftly on its own behalf.

On 28 July, member William Bentley recorded in his diary that the beacon "was raised by a large & Jovial party of our Mariners." According to Bentley, it was a conical structure, fifty-seven feet tall and crowned by a ball two feet in diameter, "painted black, except a part of the top which was neglected and remains white." A "convenient room" was housed in the lower part with a door in the south, "narrow & painted red, as is the building, but the battens at the door, white, that it might more easily be found." No ventilation was provided other than a window one foot square. The beacon, remarked Bentley, had "an awkward effect," and the foundations were "very miserably laid." Even more surprising than this amateur effort was the fact that the society had not considered that this dark unlighted structure would be useless at night. They soon realized their error, petitioned Congress for a lighthouse, and achieved their aim in 1798 (see chapter 2). They also petitioned Congress for reimbursement of their expenses for the beacon, but in this case without success.[21]

Marine societies often took the lead in lobbying for the establishment of new lighthouses. Before the Revolution, eleven lighthouses were completed by the colonies, seven of them in New England. All were built at sites vitally important to navigation: Boston (1716), Brant Point, Nantucket (1746), Beavertail (1749), New London (1760), Plymouth (1768), Portsmouth (1771), and Cape Ann (1771). They had other features in common as well. They were established by colonial or local governments at the urging of local merchants and ship masters, often following a disastrous shipwreck. They were cheaply and sometimes badly built, of masonry or wood. They were usually financed with light dues collected from vessels in nearby ports, and these funds were generally inadequate for proper maintenance. In most cases, a house was provided for the keeper and his family.

Boston Lighthouse, 1716

In 1701, Clough's *New England Almanac* proposed Allerton's Point on Nantasket Island (now Hull) as a site for a lighthouse. No action was taken until 1713, when Boston merchants petitioned for "a Light Hous and Lanthorn on some Head Land at the Entrance of the Harbor of Boston for the Direction of Ships and Vessels in the Night time." A committee including experienced shipmasters, appointed by the Massachusetts General Court, recommended that "the Southernmost Part of the Great Brewster called Beacon Island is the most convenient Place for Erecting a Light House." From here a light would be visible to vessels within Massachusetts Bay and a help in negotiating the islands in Boston harbor.[22]

The light was lit 14 September 1716, from a wooden lantern atop a stone tower approximately sixty feet in height. The city was proud of its achievement, and rightfully so, for by the end of the previous century even England had only fourteen lighthouses, Ireland five, and Scotland two. The final cost, of lighthouse, lamps, keeper's dwelling, and docks, was £2,385 17s. 8d., considerably more than originally appropriated. To pay for maintenance, light dues were charged at the rate of "one Penny per Ton Inwards, and another Penny Outwards, except Coasters, who are to pay Two Shillings each at their clearance Out, and all Fishing Vessels, Wood Sloops, etc., Five Shillings each by the Year."

Maintenance of the lighthouse proved difficult. A fire (which the keeper supposed "was occasioned by ye Lamps dropping on ye wooden Benches & a snuff falling off and setting fire") caused serious damage in 1720, and repairs were needed again in 1723 and 1726. Cracks had to be sealed in 1734 and the outside encased with oak planks and bound with iron hoops. After another fire in 1751, the wooden lantern was replaced with one of metal. Apparently, this lantern was satisfactory, for it served as the model for one at New London ten years later.[23]

Confusion sometimes arises over the difference between a lantern and a lantern room. Usually we think of a single enclosed light as a lantern; originally the word was *lanthorn* because transluscent pieces of horn protected the flame from the elements. The lantern room of a lighthouse, also known simply as the lantern, is the large room at the top of the tower which encloses the optic that produces the light, whether a set of Argand lamps and reflectors, a Fresnel lens, or a modern aero beacon.

The first keeper, George Worthylake, was appointed at an annual salary of £50, with the stipulation that, should he be derelict in his duty, he would be fined £100. This admonition may not have been as absurd as it sounds, for, like his successors, Worthylake supplemented this income with earnings as a harbor pilot. His tenure was short lived, however. On 3 November 1718, his small boat capsized in Boston harbor, and he, his wife, two daughters, and a Negro slave were drowned. Benjamin Franklin, aged thirteen, was living in Boston at the time. At the behest of his brother, a printer, he memorialized the event with a ballad, "The Lighthouse Tragedy." Franklin hawked the poem about town, and, though he later called the verses "wretched," they nonetheless had a "prodigious run, because the event was recent, and had made a great noise."[24]

In July 1719, Worthylake's successor petitioned the General Court for a gallery on the seaward side of the lighthouse, to enable him to keep the glass clear of ice and snow in winter, and also for a "great gun," to answer ships in a fog. This latter was the country's first fog signal, fired in response to a cannon shot from approaching vessels.[25]

During the Revolution, the Boston light was a casualty of war. After British occupation of the city in 1774, American troops raided the island, removed the lamps, and set fire to the tower. But the British had the last word, blowing up the tower while retreating in 1776. The Americans, sorely pressed for metal, used pieces of the lantern "to supply the cannon with ladles."[26]

For a few years after the war, a temporary unlighted tower served in place of the lighthouse. A petition to the Massachusetts legislature in June 1783 led to construction of new light: a conical stone tower seventy-five feet high and twenty-four feet in diameter at the base, with walls seven and a half feet thick and an octagonal lantern eight feet wide. The tower still stands today.[27]

Brant Point Lighthouse, Nantucket, 1746

The second lighthouse of the British colonies was a mere harbor light, built by the town of Sherburne (later renamed Nantucket) to assist vessels entering the harbor—a treacherous passage with a sand bar and crooked channel. On 24 January 1746, the town voted £200 to build a wooden lighthouse on Brant Point, in the expectation "that the owners of, or others concerned with shipping, will maintain a light therein." Whalers, perhaps, supplied oil, as they had to Lumbert's beacon at Tarpaulin Cove. No house was provided for the keeper, who must have lived in the nearby town.

The light had a troubled history. It burned down in 1758, was rebuilt the following year, and blew down in March 1774 by "the most violent gust of wind that perhaps was ever known there." By this time, the town was a bustling port, and, when it was rebuilt, the colony granted the town permission to collect light dues from vessels using the port for maintenance. Thus things stood at the start of the

Revolution. The unfortunate light, however, was destroyed and rebuilt five times more in the course of its lifetime. In 1901, the sand bar having shifted permanently, the light was rebuilt at the outer harbor, where it still stands today.[28]

Beavertail Lighthouse, Newport, 1749

In 1730, fifteen merchants petitioned the Rhode Island legislature to erect a light "to prevent the loss of any vessels that shall come from Foreign Parts upon this Coast . . . either upon Point Judith, Beaver Tail, or Castle Hill, which in your wisdom shall be thought proper . . . It being for the Preservation of Navigation done in Foreign Places and even in our neighboring Governments where it has proved of a very great Advantage."[29] Newport was prospering from the triangle trade, transporting slaves, rum, and sugar between Africa, the West Indies, and North America. More than two hundred merchant ships and four hundred coasting vessels used the harbor, as did packet ships on runs to London. But eight years passed before a committee was appointed to build a light at Beavertail, and European hostilities acted out in the colonies caused further delay. In February 1749, sixty merchants again petitioned: "And now a general Peace being established, there appears as great a necessity of a Light-House as ever, several misfortunes having very lately happened for want thereof."[30] A new committee was appointed, and this time the lighthouse was completed by the end of the year.

Peter Harrison, colonial architect and brother of committee member Joseph Harrison, took part in construction of the lighthouse. He had recently completed Newport's Redwood Library and was later to build Touro Synagogue. The tower was wooden and was described by a contemporary observer: "The diameter at the base is 24 feet, and at the top 13 feet. The height from the top of the ground to the cornice is 58 feet, round which is a gallery, and within that stands the lanthorn, which is about 11 feet high, and 8 feet diameter. The ground the lighthouse stands on is about 12 feet above the surface of the sea at high water."[31]

Abel Franklin, a member of the lighthouse committee, was appointed keeper. Should the keeper fail in his duty, the committee was empowered "to remove him, and put another in his Room from time to time. And said Keeper shall carefully and diligently attend his duty at all times, in kindling the Lights from Sun setting to Sun rising, and placing them so as they may be most seen by vessels coming into or going out from this Colony."[32]

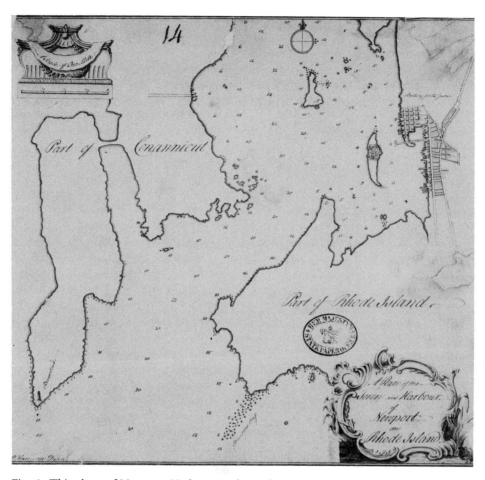

Fig. 8. This chart of Newport Harbor was drawn by Peter Harrison in 1755 and includes the earliest known portrayal of Beavertail Lighthouse. Courtesy of the Public Record Office, London.

In 1753, Beavertail Lighthouse burned to the ground—as was often the case with early lighthouses. This time the General Assembly wasted no time and ordered a new one of stone or brick, "at the place where that lately burnt stood." The tower and dwelling were completed the next spring at a cost of nearly £4,500, again with Harrison's help. Only two years later, however, a committee was appointed "to put the light house in good repair," first indication of problems that plagued the light for the rest of its lifetime. It is something of a puzzle, considering Harrison's stature, why the light needed repairs so frequently; perhaps any tall rubble stone tower would have had problems with cracks and leaking, given the technical limitations of the time.[33] When replaced a century later, Beavertail was considered one of the worst-built lighthouses in New England. The old foundation can still be seen as the base of the present fog signal.

Other problems plagued the light. In Massachusetts, the island for the Boston Lighthouse had been ceded to the colony by the town of Hull. Beavertail Point, however, had been allocated to Benedict Arnold in 1659 when the colonists purchased the island from the Indians. When the light was built, the legislature attempted to appropriate the land from the Arnold family. Petitions from Josiah Arnold tell something of what followed. In 1754, he wrote, the General Assembly proposed "to take from me, and set apart, without my consent, a part and parcel of my Estate" for the purpose of the light. Though strenuously objecting, Arnold agreed the following year to take on "charge and oversight" of the lighthouse in order "to preserve peace and quiet and secure my estate from the inroads and ravages of disorderly people." Under this arrangement, Arnold himself appointed "a proper person to make and tend the light," accepting from the colony £18 15s. annually for the keeper's salary, "though it was a sum in no way adequate." Arnold next found himself blamed by merchants and seamen for the dimness of the light, even though the problem "was caused by the bad construction of the lanthorn . . . darkened by the smoke that arose from the lamps for want of a proper Funnell to discharge it." In 1760, the assembly appointed a committee, including Arnold and Harrison, to alter the lantern. Arnold sent his son to Boston to make a model of the lantern there, "that ours might be properly constructed from it." The model was approved, but no money was forthcoming, and "the needful alteration was unhappily put off." The model nonetheless was put to good use: "Some gentlemen from New London appointed to Build a Light House there highly approved of this model and procured it and constructed a complete Lanthorn therefrom." Four years later, funds were appropriated for Beavertail, the lantern was altered, and complaints stopped.[34]

During the Revolution, the tower was damaged when the approaching French fleet forced the British from Newport. William Ellery later described the incident and its consequences: "The British . . . set fire to it and the flames so shocked the walls; especially about the Windows, that, notwithstanding they are four feet and a half thick at the bottom and three and a half feet thick at the top, our Masons have not since been able to make them tight and secure against the impression of storms of rain."[35] In 1783, the General Assembly voted a tax on shipping to raise funds for the repair of the lighthouse.

New London Lighthouse, 1760

New London was Connecticut's chief port, much smaller than its competing neighbors, Newport, Boston, and New York. Vessels using the harbor were mainly engaged in trade with the West Indies and coastal trade from Newfoundland to Georgia. At the time the light was built, the harbor resembled the idyllic landscape described a century later:

> The mouth of the [Thames River] lies directly open to Long Island Sound. It has no intricate channel, no extensive shoals or chains of islands, to obstruct the passage, but presents to view a fair, open port, inviting every passing sail, by the facility of entrance and security of anchorage, to drop in and enjoy her accomodations. The harbour is a deep, spacious and convenient basin; abounding in choice fish, and its margin furnished with sandy beaches, finely situated for the enjoyment of sea air and sea bathing.[36]

In 1760, the Connecticut Legislature authorized a lottery to finance the colony's first official lighthouse, which was to cost £500. The completed structure was of dressed masonry, sixty-four feet high, twenty-four feet in diameter, with four-foot walls at the base. It was built on a rocky ledge on the west side of the harbor, and its wooden lantern, as we have seen, was modeled on a miniature of the one at Boston. A committee was appointed to oversee its management, but, as elsewhere, maintenance proved more expensive than anticipated. In 1774, light dues were raised to cover costs, and a member of the committee was reimbursed £20 for his own money spent on the light.[37]

In 1791, the light was illuminated by three spider lamps—pans of oil with wicks around the edge—with three spouts each, consuming eight hundred gallons of strained spermaceti oil annually. In 1799, a ten-foot crack appeared in the wall.

This, and decay of the wooden lantern, led to a decision to rebuild. The new tower was completed in 1801 at a cost of $16,500, and the light is still in service today.[38]

Plymouth Lighthouse, 1768

On 17 February 1768, the General Court of Massachusetts authorized the building of a lighthouse on Gurnet Point off Plymouth, on land owned by John and Hanna Thomas.[39] In July of that year, it requested the Boston Marine Society "to take a Sirvey [sic] of Plymouth Harbour in order to give Directions for Sailing in and out by a New Light House which is to be Erected their [sic]." Lighted the same year, this was the first American "twin" light: a dwelling of thirty feet by fifteen feet with towers thirty feet high at either end, two lamps and four wicks in each. Its cost was £660. The colony paid rent of five shillings a year to Thomas and hired him as keeper for £200. Hannah succeeded as keeper on his death.

In 1801, the lighthouse burned to the ground, and the merchants of Plymouth and Duxbury erected a temporary replacement. The following year, the federal government built a new twin light, with wooden towers twenty-two feet high spaced thirty feet apart. But mariners complained that, as they neared the light, the two beams merged and appeared as one, causing confusion with the single Barnstable light nearby. In 1843, the light was rebuilt as two wooden towers thirty-nine feet in height, this time thirty-one feet apart. Complaints continued, but nothing was done until 1924, when the northeast tower was discontinued and later removed. The remaining tower is still active today.

Cape Ann Lighthouse, 1771

The last lighthouse to be built before the Revolution was on Thacher's Island, one mile off Cape Ann on the sea lanes from Europe. The island and a treacherous reef to the south, the Londoner, had caused the wreck of many a vessel. The first recorded New England shipwreck occurred here in 1635, a tragedy movingly recorded by the Rev. Anthony Thacher; he and his wife were the only survivors. Thacher was journeying from Ipswich to Marblehead to set up a new congregation when the vessel on which they were sailing broke up in a storm. The two washed ashore on the island while twenty-three others, mostly family members, perished. Out of compassion, the government of Massachusetts deeded the island to Thacher.[40]

In 1771, at the urging of merchants of Marblehead, the colony authorized a lighthouse on the island, and on 2 December the twin towers, forty-five feet high and three hundred feet apart, were lighted.[41] The first keeper, Captain James Kirkwood, was promised a salary of "100 pounds, 6 shillings and firewood" and the help of two assistants. Collection of dues was difficult as vessels were already paying tolls for lights at Boston and Plymouth, and, after eighteen months of work, Kirkwood had received only his provisions. At the onset of the Revolution, he was accused of being a Tory and fled to Canada. The towers remained dark for several years thereafter.

The Revolution marked a time of destruction to the fledgling string of colonial lighthouses,* and, following conclusion of the war in 1783, the states began repairing their damaged structures. Massachusetts, in addition, built new lights at Great Point on Nantucket in 1784 and at Newburyport in 1788 and in 1790 began work on the Portland Head light (this at a time when Maine was still part of the Commonwealth). This was to be the final state financing of lighthouse construction, as we shall see, for the new nation in 1789 assumed responsibility for its navigational aids, along with many other pressing and unwieldy problems.

*In addition to the early southern New England lighthouses mentioned in this chapter, colonial lights were built at Portsmouth, New Hampshire (1771), Sandy Hook, New Jersey (1764), Cape Helopen, Delaware (1767), Charleston, South Carolina (1767), and Tybee Island, Georgia (1748?).

The Struggle for a System

Perhaps I should on this occasion vow to build a chapel to some saint; but . . . if I were to vow at all, it should be to build a better lighthouse.

—BENJAMIN FRANKLIN, following a near shipwreck on
his second voyage to England.

On 7 August 1789, the new Congress, in its ninth act and first public works legislation, declared "that all expenses . . . in the necessary support, maintenance and repairs of all lighthouses, beacons, buoys and public piers erected, placed, or sunk before the passing of this act, at the entrance of, or within any bay, inlet, harbor, or port of the United States, for rendering the navigation thereof easy and safe, shall be defrayed out of the Treasury of the United States."[1] In choosing to fund navigational aids through a general appropriation rather than taxing passing vessels for the use of each light, Congress established the principal of equal protection for all those sailing the coasts. But, while symbolically this act ended local control of facilities meant for the good of all, in reality it was sixty-three years before this ideal came to pass. Not until 1852 did Congress recognize that lighthouses were best managed by a body devoted solely to that purpose.

In 1789, lighthouses were among the least of the young nation's worries. The country, wrote George Washington at the time of his inauguration, faced "an ocean of difficulties, without that competency of political skills, abilities, and inclinations which is necessary to manage the helm."[2] The Constitution had been accepted by the narrowest of margins. A population of nearly four million was scattered through a country larger than any in Europe, linked only by barely passable roads and the sea. With few institutions, a large debt, and an empty Treasury, the task of starting a new government was immense.

Civil service positions were created to run the new government, and collectors of customs were appointed as agents of the Treasury Department in major ports. President Washington himself decided that lighthouses should be supervised by the collectors in the districts where the lights were located. This was logical at the time, as the only other government agencies existing were the departments of War and State, and lighthouses contributed to the revenues raised through commerce. The position of collector was important, and to fill these posts Washington chose men he knew were trustworthy.[3] Benjamin Lincoln and Jedidiah Huntington, the collectors for Boston and New London, had served with Washington as generals in the Revolution, and Newport's William Ellery had signed the Declaration of Independence.[4] When fulfilling lighthouse duties, the collectors used the title superintendent of lighthouses.

Alexander Hamilton, as secretary of the Treasury, was in charge of the collectors, but he knew no more than they about the requirements of operating lighthouses. Fifteen lights stood in 1789, two more having been completed by Massachusetts and one by Virginia since the Revolution. Massachusetts was the only state with more than one—the Commonwealth boasted six—but even here there was no coordination of such matters as purchase of supplies or supervision of keepers. In Massachusetts as elsewhere, record keeping was haphazard, and no one seemed to know what the lighthouses cost to build and operate.

By the end of 1789, Hamilton had asked the customs collectors to visit the lights in their districts and report on their status to him. William Ellery reported that the whole expense of the Newport Lighthouse for one year was "nearly $445" and that the keeper for several years, William Martin, was "well qualified for the business."[5] From Boston, Deputy Collector John Rice wrote that one lighthouse and one beacon were maintained there by the Commonwealth but that the money collected was insufficient and the lighthouse considerably in debt. While the beacon cost little to maintain, "being only something like a mast, [and] sometimes washed away by the sea," repair of the wharves and boats used for pilotage was considerably more.[6] Supplies for the last two years, he continued, included three tons of oil, fifty pounds of cotton wick yarn, twenty-five cords of wood, sixty bushels of charcoal, and one hundred pounds of candles. He commended the present keeper, Thomas Knox, as "a man of capacity and reputation [who] I believe will execute the Duties of the office with fidelity and honor if he obtains the appointment."[7]

Benjamin Lincoln inspected the outlying lighthouses in his Boston district and found problems that he had not anticipated. He wrote Hamilton that he had hoped Newburyport's twin lights would not need repairs, "as they are but three or four years old"; inspection showed, however, that "the boards, being exposed to the sun, shrink so as to leave the building very open and exposed to the storms and the wet and will soon injure the timbers, and the houses without attention will in a short time fall into decay and ruin." To shingle and paint them would cost about £41.[8]

The following year, Lincoln visited the twin lights at Plymouth and reported that "without immediate attention they must be lost." The flat wooden roof had been covered with lead, but during the war it had been "wontonly destroyed" by a garrison stationed there. What was left, he declared, had "suffered much injury by the wasting hand of time." Repairs would cost $170. The keeper, Lincoln reported, was Mr. Thomas, son of the late General Thomas, whose mother previously had cared for the light. "When she was first appointed to that trust he was a minor, otherwise he probably would have had the appointment himself."[9] Hannah Thomas was the first woman to serve as a lighthouse keeper in the United States.

In addition to such information gleaned by the collectors, other advice was offered to the government about its lights. The Boston Marine Society wrote President Washington that not a single buoy marked Boston harbor, and only one beacon. Moreover, "there ought to be two active and vigilant people to attend the light during the four months of winter when the nights are very long and snow and storms frequent which renders an attention to the exterior sides of the lanthorn necessary to prevent an obscuring of the lights by the snow."[10] Peleg Cotton, Nantucket's Great Point keeper, informed the Treasury that in the past "the Commonwealth provided a large signal flag and broad pendant to be hoisted in case of distress of any ship or vessel on or near the shoals which is ofttimes the case; and immediate relief is had from the town." The flag was worn out, he reported, and needed replacing.[11] There is no evidence that the government heeded such requests; as the Treasury was nearly empty, it is not likely that it did.[12]

Initially, both Washington and Hamilton made decisions about the lights, approving expenditures and appointing keepers. Washington also wished to establish a rational basis for determining salaries, which had ranged between $80 and $400 per year when paid by the states. By 1793, Washington had reached a decision on the issue of keepers' wages, which were to be adjusted according to the rising cost of living, and in some cases because of the advantages or difficulties of the keeper's situation. The keepers at New York, Boston, and Thacher's Island would earn the

Fig. 9. Early view of Boston light with the keeper standing in the doorway. Note the docking area needed for his work as the harbor pilot. Courtesy of the National Archives.

same as those at Charleston, Cape Henry, and Cape Henlopen: $266⅔ per annum, "and nothing whatsoever found them for their own use or provision." The keeper at Plymouth was to earn $200; those at Conanicut (Newport) and Portland Head $160, and the keeper at New London $120. The salaries at Boston, Thacher's Island, and Plymouth were being reduced, the latter because of "the country being very fertile and fish plenty and cheap," and the first two because of "very convenient opportunity to pursue a profitable calling [pilotage] and . . . fish in plenty and some advantages from the land." In communicating the government's decision, Commissioner of the Revenue Tench Coxe concluded optimistically, "The present incumbents it is presumed will perceive the perfect reasonableness and equity of this reform by the President. It is but justice to assure them no representation in the smallest degree unfavorable to them has been recognized nor is anything known derogatory to their character or capacity for the service."[13]

Not surprisingly, not all keepers agreed. Thomas Knox at the Boston light wrote his collector Benjamin Lincoln that "considering the situation of the place it cannot be properly kept for the sum." For three generations, members of the Knox family had served simultaneously as keeper and chief pilot of the harbor. After the Revolution was won, explained Knox, the State of Massachusetts erected a new lighthouse "and other buildings to accomodate the keeper and pilots thereon. My grandfather being dead and my father's advanced age and loss of health forbid his discharging the duties of the office, myself then was appointed keeper. My two brothers joined with me as pilots."[14]

Then politics entered the picture. When Knox had accepted his commission from the president, he continued, "I lost the friendship of Governor Hancock [an anti-Federalist], who gave the pilotage to another," even though it was "thought that the pilotage was an emolument belonging to the keepers," and Knox had "two sons who had been regularly bred to the business."[15] Worse yet, Hancock had ordered the boat used by Knox, as property of the state, to be taken away from the island.[16] Knox figured his previous salary of $225 plus twenty-five cords of wood would equal $400 at present rates, and the wood now an additional $100. Lincoln forwarded Knox's letter to the Treasury Department with his endorsement, but the salary remained as President Washington had set it.

Washington also decided on the compensation of the collectors of customs for their work as superintendents of lighthouses: 1 percent of the annual lighthouse expenditures in their districts. This amount varied considerably from district to district. In 1792, Huntington earned $3.40, Ellery $5.80, and Lincoln $54, while collectors in New York and Philadelphia mysteriously ended up with $400.[17] Ellery and others complained about their niggardly compensation, Ellery writing his superior Alexander Hamilton, "I have spent a year of great perplexity in the public service, and unless an allowance is made for my services it will, on my part, have been spent for naught and in vain. Justice to myself and my family will not permit such sacrifices."[18] In support of the collectors' plea, Tench Coxe wrote Hamilton that "one per cent upon those small expenditures is no compensation for little troublesome services and in some instances the business has been imperfectly attended to." He noted that Army quartermasters received 5 percent for supplies and probably would work for no less. But for the next twenty-five years the commission for lighthouse supervision remained at 1 percent.[19]

In 1792, Hamilton, immersed in other matters, delegated oversight of lighthouses to the newly created position of commissioner of the revenue. Tench Coxe, the first to fill the office, was conscientious about his lighthouse duties. In communicating with the collectors, for instance, he passed on advice he considered helpful.

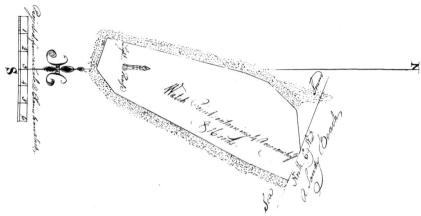

Fig. 10. 1808 plot map drawn by surveyors establishing a site for Watch Hill Lighthouse, Westerly, Rhode Island. Courtesy of the National Archives New England Region.

On 2 August 1793, he approved the request of Huntington to paint the New London Lighthouse, adding,

> It will be well to proceed on the business during this favorable season. The days are of great length and the weather will be long suitable for drying the painting about the windows. I recommend the white wash to be made out of the best mortar mixed with hair, diluted only so far as to render it capable of application by brush. It is said that a quart of new milk thrown into each bucket of white wash at the time of making it, will give it a tenacity and a capacity to resist moisture.[20]

Coxe was also involved in review of proposals for new lighthouses. On 18 February 1793, a petition was presented to Congress from "a number of inhabitants of Connecticut and Rhode Island praying that a lighthouse be erected at the expense of the United States on Watch Hill."[21] In May of the following year, Coxe addressed the following questions to the customs collectors of the area:

> Is another lighthouse necessary in that quarter wherein there are already two lighthouses, at New London and Conanicut, and wherein Montauk is authorized? Is Watch Hill the most suitable place? What kind or size is desirable?

How far should the light be visible? What is the distance from Fisher's Island
to the mainland, and what is the width of the channel for decked vessels?
What is the extent of shoals or ledges in that passage, and are the shoals,
ledges or single rocks numerous? What height above high water is the site? Is
the rise and fall of tides rapid or otherwise? What are the distances from the
five nearest families and what is the nature of the vicinity as to fertility, pov-
erty of soils, cultivation, and what other traders besides those through the
channel of Fisher's Island will be accomodated by it?

Coxe concluded by asking for an accurate drawing of the coast from Rhode Island
to New London, including the east end of Long Island.[22]

On 8 December 1794, Coxe reviewed a letter from fifty-five shipmasters and
owners in favor of Gull Island as a site. The choice of Watch Hill was defended on
the other hand by George Stillman, surveyor of the Port of Pawcatuck. The dispute
was finally settled on 22 January 1806 when President Jefferson authorized two lighthouses, one at Watch Hill and the other at Sand's Point in Northampsted, New
York. The light at Watch Hill was finally lit in 1808.

Other New England lights erected before the end of the century included Baker's
Island, Cape Cod, and Gay Head. All were important to navigation and had been
long urged by merchants, mariners, and related organizations. Often, however,
Congress did not act until tragedy made a new light imperative.

In 1792, the Salem Marine Society petitioned Congress for a light at the north
end of Baker's Island, but, three years later, no action had been taken. In 1796, the
loss of three vessels and sixteen lives in one month finally spurred Congress to
authorize $6,000.[23] Several prominent Salem citizens offered their services to Coxe:
"As we are desirous to forward a work of singular utility to ourselves, and to the
states, we are ready to answer any questions." They described the barren island as
having a high, rocky shore and no meadows and proudly stated that information
in hand on the island's bearings and distance from surrounding islands was based
on "an actual survey of 1794 . . . reported by gentlemen of liberal education, and
we believe of distinguished accuracy. An excellent theodilite and quadrants were
employed by different hands and the mean of all the observations were taken."[24]

Supervision of the lighthouse was assigned to Benjamin Lincoln, whose lighthouse duties were expanding beyond the port of Boston. Concerned that the new
light might be confused with others nearby, Lincoln proposed that it be built as a
triple light with three stone pillars spaced evenly along a flat-roofed keeper's house,
fifty feet in length. This, he believed, with twin lights at Thacher's and Plymouth,

Fig. 11. Baker's Island Lighthouse, from a chart of Salem Harbor drawn by Nathaniel Bowditch in 1804. Courtesy of the Peabody Museum of Salem.

separated by a single light at Boston and another single planned for Cape Cod, would give sailors good guidance at night. Meanwhile, however, the Treasury Department had decided on an eclipsing light for Cape Cod, and the Baker's Island light was built as a wooden house, forty feet long, with a light at each end. To prevent confusion with the twin lights at Plymouth, the towers were of different heights, ninety-five and seventy-eight feet.

George Chapman, a member of the Salem Marine Society, was appointed keeper. For his compensation, Lincoln recommended to Coxe a salary of $266⅔, the same as that of the keeper of Seguin Island, Maine, plus ten acres of land for his own use. Regarding the two situations, he commented, "I hardly know which has the most advantages or the greatest number of evils to combat. . . . Baker's Island is three miles from any place from whence the keeper can get his necessary supplies and in blowing or very cold weather is excluded from any communication with the mainland. N.B.: There is no wood on the island, it must be purchased at Salem." Needed would be a "proper boat and means for drawing her upon the land clear of the surf, and . . . a barn. . . . Fencing will also be requisite for dividing the land belonging to the lighthouse from other parts of the island." He concluded by assuring Coxe that he would instruct the keeper "that economy in the expenditure of public stock is an object which requires a particular attention of all the servants in the union." Lincoln requested the Salem Marine Society to publish new sailing directions for Salem Harbor. They appeared in the *Salem Gazette* on 19 December, and on 3 January 1798 the Baker's Island lamps were lighted.[25]

The need for a light on Cape Cod had been discussed for years. In 1797, petitions from the marine societies of Boston and Salem, the Salem Chamber of Commerce, and the Massachusetts Humane Society finally led to approval by Congress.

With the help of the Boston Marine Society, Lincoln selected a ten-acre site at Clay Ponds near Truro, which at 150 feet was one of the highest spots on the eastern Cape. He wrote Coxe of its advantages: fresh water was easily obtained, the land could summer a cow, and the nearest families were within a fourth of a mile.[26] Twin lights had already been suggested for Cape Cod, yet, as there were already twins at Cape Ann and at Newburyport, Lincoln proposed as an alternative two lights in the same tower, one ten or fifteen feet above the other. The Boston Marine Society, however, advocated that an eclipsing mechanism be added to a single light, stating "that one light would be best and would answer every purpose, provided it was so constructed as to be seen one Minute and hid from the sight the next minute and so on alternately." Coxe accepted this advice, and thus was established the first eclipsing light in the United States.

In obtaining an eclipser, Lincoln hoped that Coxe would use "American talent" rather than send to England for the device and urged him to employ a John Bailey, Jr., "whom I consider the first mechanical genius in this state."[27] Coxe agreed to Bailey's services for an eclipser to "perform one revolution in 80 seconds, so light will be discovered about 50 seconds and eclipsed 30 seconds."[28] The eclipser operated

Fig. 12. Only known print of the first lighthouse at Gay Head, Martha's Vineyard, drawn by J. W. Barber, 1838. Courtesy of the Dukes County Historical Society.

by means of a clockwork mechanism that caused an opaque shield to cover the light at regular intervals.

But time passed, and Lincoln, fearing that Bailey might not finish his work in time for the scheduled lighting, wrote in alarm to Coxe, "An eclipser could not be expected soon from Europe or elsewhere, and learning from masters of ships, pilots, and others, the best informed in these matters, that there would be the utmost hazard in establishing a light on Cape Cod without something by which it could be distinguished from Boston light."[29] Fortunately, Bailey did complete the work in time. Sailing directions were prepared by the Boston Marine Society with help from a branch pilot for the port of Boston and two residents of Cape Cod. They were issued on 2 January 1798, and on 15 January 1798 the light was lit, shining two hundred feet above the sea.[30]

In 1798, Congress appropriated $5,750 for a light for Gay Head, the first on Martha's Vineyard. In June of the following year, the New Bedford collector, Edward Pope, advertised for bids for an octagonal wooden tower twenty-four feet at the base and forty-seven feet high. The lantern was to be six feet in diameter and seven feet high, with "a good circular lamp of two feet in diameter." A house for the keeper would also be built, seventeen feet by twenty-six feet, with a parlor, kitchen, and bedroom, plus a barn fifteen feet square, an underground oil vault, and a well. Martin Lincoln, son of the Boston customs collector, won the contract with a low bid of $2,875.[31]

Though Coxe had been concerned that a light at Gay Head would be confused with those at Nantucket and Montauk Point, the problem was still not resolved as construction was completed. Coxe's successor, William Miller, suggested adding a second light: "I presume that a lamp of double the size of the common street lamp and capable of holding sufficient oil to burn through the night might be raised from the trap door of the dwelling. . . . it should be well oiled to prevent it from rusting."[32] If such a solution was tried, no record of it has been found. A single fixed light was lit on 18 November 1798.

Ebenezer Skiff was appointed keeper at a salary of $200 per year. Apparently, he received no training, for the following October he explained why he was using more oil than formerly: "Being unexperienced at first I made the wicks too small which consumed less oil." In no way did Skiff have an easy time in his post. The house lacked storage space for iron ware and water vessels, and the cellar was "half-full of water for most of the winter and spring." In 1803, Skiff complained to Pope that his salary was insufficient, and the Chilmark selectmen certified that Skiff

> dwells about four miles from the nearest family of white people, six miles from a district school, nine miles from the meetinghouse and nearly the same distance from a gristmill—the way is hilly and bad and in the common way of passing there are creeks which are scarcely fordable at all seasons. The spring in the Clift where he dwells yields poor water at best and will not afford a sufficiency for a family. In dry seasons he has to cart water from a brook nearly one mile distant—his firewood must be brought by water and is not so easily obtained there as in seaport towns—his situation is uncommonly boisterous and the pasturage which he is obliged to hire of the natives is generally very inconvenient.

Even this appeal brought him no increase. But two years later he wrote directly to Albert Gallatin, now secretary of the Treasury, and his salary was finally raised to $250 a year.[33]

By 1800, twenty-four lighthouses marked the coast. By any standard, singly and together they failed in their primary purpose of guiding ships safely at night. The

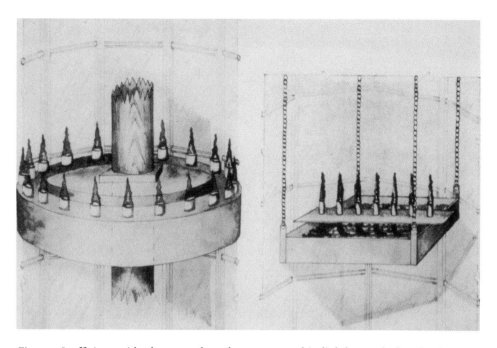

Fig. 13. Inefficient spider lamps such as these were used in lighthouses before development of Argand lamps with reflectors. U.S. Coast Guard, *Aids-to-Navigation Manual*, 1945.

technical knowledge needed to make bright, steady lights was sorely lacking, and the problem of distinguishing one from another remained unsolved. Few of the customs collectors were conscientious in supervising the keepers, and they themselves lacked direction from the Treasury Department. Building contracts were awarded to the lowest bidder, and supplies, purchased locally, were often inferior. Whale oil was often smokey and hard to ignite at cold temperatures, and controlling its quality seemed beyond the capacity of the government. Finally, without a single government authority on lighthouse matters, few mechanisms existed to disseminate improvements from one district to another.

Technical improvements were occasionally attempted. One cause of dim lights was poor ventilation of the lantern rooms, causing soot and moisture to collect on windows, walls, and ceiling. In 1790, Boston's Lincoln thought that he had found a solution. He wrote Hamilton:

One of the great evils which . . . has prevented [lighthouses] being as extensively useful as they might have been [is] . . . from want of some method either to carry off or annihilate the smoking that has generally fallen on the glass and greatly obscured the light. . . . No person could be constantly employed during the whole night, in cleaning them for they would soon have been suffocated. The daily complaints of the badness of our light at the entrance of Boston harbor led me to attempt a remedy by an alteration of the lantern and by a different construction of the lamps.

As the lantern room was presently designed, he continued, smoke was supposed to exit through an opening in the roof, partly covered to keep out the rain and snow. A vane attached to the covering was intended to keep the opening to leeward, but the vane frequently got stuck, and "keepers have been obliged at all times of the night at the utmost hazard in going upon the outside of the lantern to turn the head by hand." To remedy this, Lincoln substituted a copper plate for the cover and made small holes in the roof and sides of the lantern to facilitate the movement of air. He redesigned the lamp as a circular plate, three feet in diameter and divided in quarters, with

a hole in the center for air to ascend. By the openings at the bottom there is a constant accession of fresh air which circulating through the opening in the plate and the space between the glass and the lamps extends the blaze, and gives that, and the smoke, a proper direction to its escape. Besides these lamps have another advantage, by throwing the light so much together it keeps the oil sufficiently warm, and precludes the necessity of burning coals in winter in the lantern, to prevent the oil from chilling.[34]

Whatever the improvement this may have worked at Boston, the advantages of Lincoln's design were not implemented elsewhere, at least not outside Lincoln's district. The following year, Joseph Whipple, the collector at Portsmouth, New Hampshire, wrote Hamilton of a fire in that light due partly to faulty construction of the vessel, "in use many years," containing the oil. Whipple thought that the fish oil in use at the Portsmouth light gave "a very indifferent light," but his substituting a better oil caused the fire to break out, probably from the more intense heat of the new fuel.[35] In any case, problems with ventilation plagued the lights for decades.

Technical solutions were elsewhere slow in coming. When a light was established at Watch Hill in 1808, its signal was distinguished with an eclipser. The following year, the eclipser stopped, and the keeper, Jonathan Nash, wrote to the superintendent for his district to ask what he should do. William Ellery replied that he had received no complaints:

> This stoppage of the eclipser was without doubt owing to the clockwork of it having become foul. You should procure a phial of clear . . . oil, keep it in some safe warm place in your house, examine the clockworks now and then; and if you find any rust gathering on any part of it, dip a feather into the phial, and lightly touch the rusting part with the oil; and any other part of it which may want oil.[36]

It is doubtful that this solved Nash's immediate problem, and Watch Hill was considered a particularly bad light for many years.[37]

The lot of the keepers was a hard one. For their tedious work they got little help, and often much criticism. Officials in Washington who decided their salaries and other conditions of living had little understanding of their duties or sympathy for the hardships endured. That so many sought out the work suggests how few alternatives there were.

The experience of Matthew Mayhew, for thirty-three years the keeper of Cape Poge Lighthouse on Martha's Vineyard, illustrates the difficulties encountered at a remote station.[38] The wooden tower and keeper's house, fifteen feet by thirty-two feet, had been built for a modest $2,000 in 1801.[39] Mayhew was appointed keeper soon after by President Jefferson at a salary of $200. Though New Bedford was the port where most Vineyarders went for supplies, Mayhew was placed under the jurisdiction of the Boston collector, Lincoln. The nearest town, Edgartown, was five miles distant. Because the walk was arduous, Mayhew asked for a boat. His request was granted.

In 1804, Mayhew wrote the secretary of the Treasury, Albert Gallatin, requesting a fence.

> The place where [the light] stands is sandy. The sheep and cattle that come round it for shade keep the sand loose and the high winds which are frequent

and continually blowing away the sand [so] that in a short time it will endanger the foundations of the house. Believing it to be for the public interest as well as some profit to me, I wish if it should be judged best, that the land may be fenced. This is the only thing that will keep the sheep and cattle from undermining the foundation of the house.

This time, three years passed before his request was granted.[40]

Mayhew's family was growing—ultimately it numbered eight children—and in 1812 he asked for a larger boat. When no action followed, a local customs officer wrote on his behalf to the Boston collector, Henry Dearborn, stating that the old vessel was not worth repairing and that "it is absolutely necessary that Mayhew should be furnished with one as his local situation is such that he cannot do without a new Boat." Dearborn forwarded the request to Gallatin, and eventually a new boat was supplied, but the same size as the old.[41]

In 1812, Mayhew asked for an addition to his house: "The dwelling house is small and ilconvenient, their is but tow small rooms without any place to put our iron ware, we are obliged to put it up garet or down sellar and but one way outdoors except we pass out of the window which is offen the case. In storme weather the house is so small that it is not in my power to acomedat peopel that comes hear by distress of weather."[42] It was not until 1816, however, after conclusion of the war with England, that an addition of fourteen feet by fourteen feet was built and, at the same time, the dwelling and lighthouse were painted for the first time in fifteen years. Mayhew requested that a door be included in the addition, for during storms the "family frequently are obliged to have the wood and water, etc., past in at one of the lee windows on account of the difficulty attending the opening of the door."[43]

After the stormy winter of 1825, Mayhew informed Dearborn that, since he had become keeper, the land at the lighthouse had been reduced from four acres to two:

The land washes away very fast. The distance from the dwelling house to the edge of the bank is 40 feet. I have known 14 feet of the bank to wash away in one tide. Consequently, it is my opinion that it would be expediant for the dwelling House to be moved the present Summer. If we are not in danger of falling immediately down the clift, it is very unpleasant, particular to females to be thus situated in storms when the Sea is beating with such violance as for the spray to fly against and over the House and no other dwelling House within 5 miles for a refuge. Should it meet your approbation and will have it accomplished, it would be very gratifying.[44]

For once the government acted quickly. Four additional acres were purchased and the house moved, all within two months.

Mayhew died on 20 December 1834, age "about 69," serving as keeper to the end. Neither of his sons sought to succeed him, which was not surprising, considering the difficulties of life at Cape Poge. But a new keeper did not arrive until 12 January. Six days earlier, a schooner bound from New York to Boston was wrecked on the shore, and three passengers froze to death. Absence of a light may well have contributed to the tragedy.

After the turn of the century, as the number of lights increased, the problems were compounded. There was still no one really in charge, and responsibility continued to be shifted. In 1802, Jefferson abolished the position of commissioner of the revenue and transferred lighthouses back to the secretary of the Treasury; but with the next administration, in 1813, they again reverted to the commissioner of the revenue. In 1820, as part of a general reorganization of the civil service, Congress created a new office to deal exclusively with lighthouses and other navigational aids. But lighthouses were still perceived as a bureaucratic, not navigational, matter. Appointed to this position of fifth auditor of the Treasury was career bureaucrat Stephen Pleasonton, a man with no maritime experience at all. He held this post for thirty-two years, the darkest period for America's lighthouses.[45]

3

The Darkest Years

It ought never to be forgotten, that the indiscriminate erection of lighthouses soon leads to confusion and the needless
exhibition of a light, by involving the loss of a distinction,
may afterwards prove inconvenient in the case of some future light, which time and the growing wants of trade may
call for on the same line of coast.

—ALAN STEVENSON, "Sea-Lights"

Viewers marveled when they first saw Argand lamps with reflectors shining forth
from the Boston lighthouse. The year was 1810, and previously only smokey spider
lamps had illuminated American lighthouses. Superior Argand lamps, used for
navigational lighting in Europe for many years, had found mainly domestic use in
the United States. Winslow Lewis, with permission of Collector of Customs Henry
Dearborn, had installed six sets of these lamps and reflectors in the lighthouse in
early May. This event marked the beginning of Lewis's long and fateful association
with the young nation's lighthouses.[1]

Lewis was born in 1770 to a Wellfleet family of preachers and shipmasters.[2] As
did his three brothers, Lewis followed the sea and for several years was master of
a packet that sailed between Boston and England.[3] At the age of twenty-seven, he
was elected to the Boston Marine Society and would serve as its president from
1818 to 1820. But Lewis was more than a mariner; he was also a shrewd businessman
and an opportunist. His ventures included part ownership in the Bemis Manufacturing Company of Watertown, Massachusetts, a firm that in 1809 became the first
American producer of cotton duck, challenging the Russian monopoly on sailcloth.
During the War of 1812, he was co-owner of a privateer, the brig *Abaelino*. In 1818,

Fig. 14. Crowninshield's Wharf, Salem, painted by M. MacPherson after a painting by George Ropes, 1806. Courtesy of the Peabody Museum of Salem.

owning a rope-making firm at the foot of the Boston Common, he bought out a competitor and soon was producing more than seven hundred tons of cordage annually valued at $18,000.[4] He was also a venture capitalist: in 1813, he financed David Melville's pioneering efforts to introduce gas lighting in American factories. As time proved, this would not be the only time that Lewis was not what he seemed.

When Jefferson's embargo of 1807 cut off trade with Europe, many seamen lost their livelihood. Perhaps this situation turned Lewis to manufacture, for, on 24 June 1808, he took out a patent for a binnacle lamp, a device long used on British ships to facilitate the reading of a ship's compass at night.[5]

On the evening of 8 May 1810, the six Argand lamps newly installed, Lewis went down to the harbor with a committee of fellow members of the Boston Marine Society and sailed several leagues into the Bay to where they could see the lighthouses of both Boston and Baker's Island. At 10:00 P.M., by prearrangement with the keeper, the regular lamps of the Boston light were extinguished and those of Lewis lighted. "The difference in the brightness of these and the Light at Baker's Island was as great as would appear between a well-trimmed Argand Lamp and a common Candle," reported the committee. Not only was Lewis's invention superior, the surprisingly well-informed report continued, but his apparatus could be installed in existing lighthouses without alteration to their structure. No more than sixteen sets would be needed in any lighthouse, and the lamps would consume only one-third

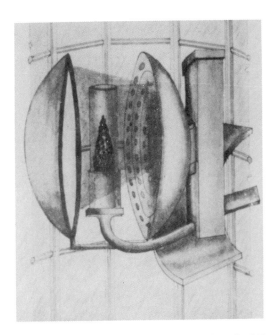

Fig. 15. Argand lamp with reflector and lens. U.S. Coast Guard, *Aids-to-Navigation Manual*, 1945.

the oil of the lamps then in use.* The Committee declared itself "highly gratified with the result and . . . of opinion that should this improved method be adopted, it would be productive of great public utility."[6]

One of the twin lights on Cape Ann was soon fitted with Lewis's apparatus, and several months later the enthusiastic Boston collector Henry Dearborn reported that the lights had been lighted every night "for two months or more" and that he was fully convinced that Lewis's system was far preferable to the existing mode both in brightness of the light and in the saving of oil. Waxing poetic, he added that "the southern one, which was lighted on Lewis's system, appeared, with the other, as a large brilliant star compared to a small common star." The Boston Marine Society also reported that Thacher's and Boston's lights were superior to any with

*Later statements gave the amount as one-half.

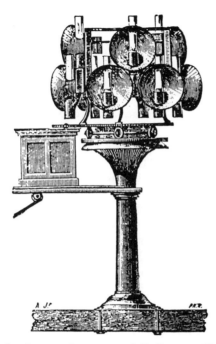

Fig. 16. Set of lamps and reflectors. Stevenson, *A Rudimentary Treatise.*

which it was familiar, and it, too, recommended adoption of Lewis's apparatus in all lighthouses along the coasts.[7]

Lamps and reflectors surely were an improvement over the spider lamps then used in U.S. lighthouses. On 24 June 1810, after his demonstrations in Boston, Lewis took out a patent (no. 1305) for a lighthouse "reflecting and magnifying lantern." His claim, however, to have invented a system of lighting already used for twenty-five years in the lighthouses of Great Britain was, of course, false. Remarkably, Congress not only paid Lewis the princely sum of $24,000 for his patent right but gave him a monopoly on lighting the country's lighthouses.

Patents at that time were easy to come by, a reversal of the strict review required by the first federal patent law of 1790. But the first patent board, which included Thomas Jefferson, was so thorough in its scrutiny that only three patents were approved during the first year. Following a relaxation of the law in 1793, until the U.S. Patent Office was established in 1836, virtually all applications for patents were approved by the government. Anyone challenging a claim to originality had to do so in the courts, and international patents were not recognized at all. This chaotic situation allowed opportunists such as Lewis to operate without restraint.[8] Production standards of course did not exist, and manufacturing capability was still primitive.[9]

Lewis's apparatus was an imitation of the Argand lamps and reflectors used in Europe since the 1780s. But the version he borrowed was already outmoded, with a thick lens in front of the lamp that once was believed to focus and intensify the rays. In fact, the lens absorbed the rays and reduced the amount of light emitted.[10] Even more critically, Lewis's reflector barely approximated the parabolic shape so critical to maximum intensification of the light.

Lewis succeeded because he promised to fill a vacuum created by the inadequate administration of navigational aids in the United States. By contrast, development of navigational aids in other countries, especially Scotland and France, shows that outstanding individuals with adequate organizational support could have a great impact on technology. In Scotland in 1786—shortly before the U.S. Congress proclaimed its responsibility for the country's lighthouses—the newly appointed Northern Lighthouse Board hired Thomas Smith as its first engineer. Smith had grown up in the port of Dundee, where his father, a ship's captain, had drowned in a wreck within sight of his home port. As a metalsmith, Smith worked to improve harbor beacons and experimented with placing a reflector behind the lamp flame to intensify the light, unaware that others were trying this elsewhere. Soon he was installing his reflector-backed lamps to light the streets of Edinburgh's New Town.[11]

Neither Smith nor the commissioners of the northern lights knew much about lighthouses when Smith was hired. First, he consulted Ezekiel Walker, an Englishman who had recently illuminated a lighthouse to the south with a single lamp and a large reflector, which he made by embedding small pieces of mirror glass in plaster lining a metal form. This reflector was an improvement over Smith's reflectors of polished tin, and the sparkling light, visible at seven leagues, was described as a flame playing "upon a great variety of pieces of glass artfully disposed, by which [it] is multiplied and reflected.[12] Smith acquired most of his expertise, however, through his own ingenuity. Within two years, by means of extraordinary powers of organization, he had erected lighthouses on four distant sites on the Scottish coast, his efforts not diminished by the fact that he could not be paid until the lights were lit and tolls collected.[13] Smith then hired as his assistant Robert Stevenson, who was to become the next pioneer of Scottish lighthouses. When Smith married

Stevenson's widowed mother and Stevenson in turn married Smith's daughter, they established a dynasty of lighthouse engineers. In the course of nearly two centuries, four generations of Stevensons built eighty-six lighthouses, some as distant as the Pacific Ocean.

Into this eminently practical family was born the Scottish romantic novelist Robert Louis Stevenson (1850–94), the only child of Robert's son Thomas. Though Louis, as he was known, tried halfheartedly to learn the family business, at the age of twenty-one he confessed to his disappointed father his ambition to become a writer. The novelist retained a deep regard for his family's often selfless labors on behalf of Scotland's lights and wrote of their undeserved anonymity,

> Holding as [they] did a government appointment, they regarded their original work as something due already to the nation, and none of them has ever taken out a patent. It is another cause of the comparative obscurity of the name: for a patent not only brings in money, it infallibly spreads reputation; and my father's instruments enter anonymously into a hundred light-rooms, and are passed anonymously over in a hundred reports, where the least considerable patent would stand out and tell its author's story.[14]

This was by no means the only time that evolution of lighthouses in Scotland compared favorably with the situation in the United States. In 1810, while Lewis was dazzling his countrymen with his purported invention, Robert Stevenson was creating a new standard for lighthouse construction on the notorious Bell Rock off Edinburgh. Here, where the wave force was measured at three thousand pounds per square foot, Stevenson not only improved on the design of the world-famous Eddystone light but also introduced innovations in lighting and fog signal technology as well as in living conditions for the lightkeepers. Especially worried about the danger of lights being confused with one another as the number increased along the coast, he bestowed a unique red and white flashing characteristic on the Bell Rock light after determining that red glass would offer less interference with transmission of light than any other color.[15] The Bell Rock Lighthouse was so advanced in every way that it became a training site for Scotland's apprentice keepers.

In Scotland, the commissioners of the northern lights worked through committees on such matters as lighthouse construction, fuel, and fog signaling. In the United States, however, lack of any oversight crippled development of an efficient, coordinated system. By the time Lewis demonstrated his apparatus, the effort to co-

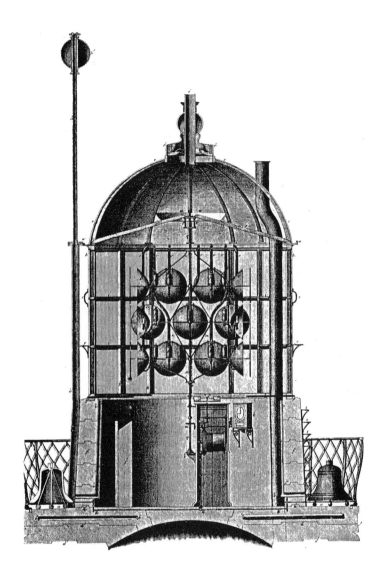

Fig. 17. Innovations introduced by Robert Stevenson at the Bell Rock Lighthouse in 1811 included a flashing red-and-white light and fog bells. Courtesy U.S. Lighthouse Society.

ordinate the characteristics of lighthouse signals had almost been abandoned. As their number grew, lights were often confused with one another.

Other Americans besides Lewis must have been familiar with the lighting technology of Great Britain, and it is striking that none challenged Lewis's claim to have invented the lamp and reflector apparatus. No doubt this was partly due to the primitive state of American technology at the time. Scientific inquiry was slow to take hold in this largely agrarian society, and the nation's scientists tended to be men such as Franklin and Jefferson who made their living in other ways.[16] Those most concerned with navigation, mariners themselves, were in no position to do more than endorse proposed improvements, and those most involved with technology seldom applied it to navigational safety. As Jeffersonian republicans gained control of the government from New England federalists, maritime matters were increasingly neglected as manifestations of an older, out-of-favor society. The government, moreover, was slow to take an active role in internal improvements. When Congress did begin to promote public works after 1810, it was by allowing army engineers to assist with the roadwork of western expansion. By the time the Lighthouse Board was established in 1852, the construction of only a handful of lighthouses had been overseen by engineers.

By 1811, with no other help in sight, secretary of the Treasury Gallatin was persuaded that Lewis's apparatus might solve the problems of the lights. The following year, on 2 March 1812, Congress authorized purchase from Lewis of his patent right "if the same shall be proved to be a discovery made by him." Lewis was to install and maintain his apparatus in all the lighthouses of the United States and to do so "for such sum as he may think for the interest of the United States, [p]rovided, the sum . . . shall not in any case annually exceed the appropriation made for supplying the lighthouse establishment with oil."[17] The sum agreed on, $24,000, was based on Lewis's claim that his apparatus would save twenty-four thousand gallons of oil annually, half that consumed by the wasteful spider lamps.[18] In addition, the government agreed to pay him $500 per year for seven years to keep the apparatus in repair, to absorb the expense of materials and of the manufacture and conveyance of the apparatus to the lighthouses, and to supply wicks and glass chimneys. Lewis for his part had to promise that his lamps and reflectors would show a more brilliant light and use only half the whale oil consumed by the old method. If they did not, he was obliged to restore the former lamps to the lighthouses and return to the government the money paid him.[19]

Lewis set to work at once, refitting his lamps and reflectors in forty lighthouses by the end of 1812. The outbreak of war with England made his work more difficult, and at Cape Poge and elsewhere his apparatus had to be hidden to be kept from enemy hands. But Lewis persevered, installing the remaining nine when hostilities ended in 1815.[20]

Lewis was performing much of this work for the first time, and it turned out that there were may unforeseen expenses. He had to have a boat, of course, and with Dearborn's blessing he purchased one of around ninety tons. He needed this well-fitted vessel, the *Federal Jack*, he later explained,

> since we were to be on the coast through every season and on the most exposed points to it. Every gale that blew on shore, we had a lee shore to contend with and often had occasion to anchor in very deep waters, which required a great length of cable. . . . On board of her was fitted a Blacksmith shop, a place suitable for the copper smith to work, and carpenter, accomodations for thirteen men, and for stowing all the apparatus and boats. There was two boats charged, the first was a light cedar-built boat for the purpose of landing our apparatus on the rocks in a rough sea, the other was a large Vineyard boat. On the coast of North Carolina many of the lights are so situated that we could not get within thirty or forty miles of them with our own vessels. This boat was calculated to carry myself and four mechanics, with all the apparatus for one lighthouse through those sounds and inlets.[21]

As it turned out, Gallatin had not approved the expenditure. When he questioned the expense, the collector—now Henry A. S. Dearborn, successor to his father and like him a Lewis supporter—forwarded Lewis's accounts to him with an apology for the fact that the purchase had been initiated by his "predecessor" without Gallatin's approval. "I regret that it is deemed improper, but presume you will be satisfied that it was from the best principles the Schooner was bought and prepared for the service required."[22]

In March of the following year, the British captured the *Federal Jack*. Lewis described the incident, and its costs, to Dearborn:

> When I engaged the officers and crew and mechanics for the *Federal Jack* to go to the southward, I could not engage them unless I obligated myself to allow them pay until they returned back to the port where they were engaged, in case of capture. They knew from the business we were a going on, that we must unavoidably fall in with the enemy. . . . We were captured on the 1st day of March, on the 5th all the men with myself was paroled except the Captain, who was detained and carried to Bermuda. We were landed at

Charleston where I hired a small vessel and sent all the men to Providence, where they arrived on the 27th March to which day their pay is made up in the Roll.[23]

Captain Brigham was paid through 6 July, the day of his return.

In addition to his lighting apparatus, Lewis furnished other supplies for the lights. The Watch Hill keeper, Jonathan Nash, reported to his superintendent on Lewis's delivery in 1813:

3 lamps
one stove
one bucket
5 wooden cisterns (estimated 200 gal. each)
5 tin butts (est. 85 gal. ea.)
2 spare lamps
2 spare illum. glasses
5 wooden trivits
2 wick boxes
12 panes of glass
15 pounds of putty
1 lantern bin
2 gal. spirits of turpentine
38 lbs. whiting
12 wick sticks
2 paint brushes
6 pounds paint
4 qts. paint oil
13½ gross wicks
14 doz. tube glasses
1½ buff skins
2 pr. shears
13 yds. cotton cloth
50 bushels charcoal

1 cord walnut wood
1 jug
1 tub
1 soldering iron
7 pounds rosin
1 pound solder
1 lantern canister
1 torch
2 tube cleaners
2 tin pans
1 file
1 pr. pincers
1 oil measure
1 diamond
2 flannel trainers
18 or thereabout bushes sea coal
one eclipser with apparatus used for keeping in motion
These articles here embraced were furnished by Winslow Lewis, also 8 lamps that are in use. The lighthouse and other buildings are in as good order as they were on the 31st day of December last, natural wear excepted.[24]

Not all keepers and collectors kept such careful records as Nash, however. At the end of the war, Lewis wrote Dearborn that he had no receipts for the goods he had delivered but promised that in the future "everything will . . . be reduced to a more regular system. The keepers' receipts will hereafter appear for every article furnished." Then he added a bill for $200: "I presume when it is recalled that in this business I have travelled several hundred miles at this inclement season that the small charge will not be objected to. It will but little more than reimburse my expense."[25]

By visiting all the lights, Lewis had become the leading authority on lighthouse matters. As he continued to install his apparatus in new lighthouses following the war, decisions were left to him concerning the characteristic of the light, the number of lamps in each, and the diameter of the reflectors, which affected how far the lights could be seen. His position gave him other opportunities to be useful as well. In 1813, he wrote Dearborn that he hoped to become sole agent for delivering oil to the lighthouses. The practice had been for collectors of the bigger ports to purchase oil at Nantucket or New Bedford and distribute it to the lights as needed. There were many abuses, including delivery of bad oil, Lewis observed to Dearborn. If he controlled delivery, he claimed, such abuses would stop.[26]

As a lighthouse fuel, whale oil posed the particular problem of congealing at temperatures below thirty degrees Farenheit. In an attempt to remedy this, the practice developed of processing oil for winter use at temperatures close to those at which it would be used. That is, the head matter of the whale was boiled in cold weather, and the particles that remained after cooling were heavier than if processed in warm weather. When strained, the oil boiled in winter was thinner than that boiled in summer and was known as "winter-pressed oil." Oil was delivered once a year, usually in the summer, and barrels marked "W" for winter-pressed oil and "S" for summer-pressed oil were left at each lighthouse.[27] But no testing was done to determine if the more expensive winter oil in fact burned at lower temperatures or even if it was the grade that suppliers claimed to deliver. If a keeper found that his oil was bad, he could request a replacement, but he usually had to wait until the next scheduled delivery before a substitute was brought. Because the oil deteriorated after a year and the casks themselves were notoriously leaky, determining quality and quantity delivered was difficult. Once again, Lewis addressed a serious problem, and the government welcomed his help.

At the end of 1815, Lewis won a lucrative new contract for distributing oil. Beginning in January 1816, and for seven years thereafter, the government agreed to deliver to Lewis, in good iron-bound casks, twenty-four thousand gallons of spermaceti oil (half summer pressed and half winter pressed) and, for any lighthouses built thereafter, an additional forty-three gallons annually for each lamp. (If any lamps were suspended, Lewis was to abate a proportionate amount of oil.) For his part, Lewis was to visit and inspect the lighthouses once a year (an easy matter, as he was delivering oil anyway) and report on their condition and on the performance of the keepers to the commissioner of the revenue. For transport of the oil (including cooperage, storage, and other incidentals), the government agreed to pay Lewis $1,200 annually, to give him the 10,500 gallons of winter oil and twelve thousand gallons of summer oil then on hand at the lighthouses, and for the remaining six years of the contract to supply him with half the oil that would have been used under the old system of lighting.[28]

Even as this new contract was beginning, however, clouds appeared on the horizon. Lewis's new lights, it appeared, were not the great improvement that he had promised. Some of the reasons were beyond his control: the lanterns still smoked up because of poor whale oil and inadequate ventilation, and untrained or inattentive keepers sometimes allowed the lights to go out at night. Lewis *was* responsible, however, for the equipment that he supplied, and his apparatus was an inferior product that could never achieve the intended purpose. For light rays to be focused most effectively, the flame had to be positioned exactly in the focus of the reflector. In 1810, to prevent any chance of misalignment, Robert Stevenson had devised a mechanism that allowed the burner to be lowered while the reflector was cleaned, then locked back in the correct position. Lewis's apparatus, however, lacked any such precision, and practices such as tipping the lamp to increase the flow of oil were common. In Scotland, manufacture of reflectors was done with particular care. Sheets of copper were bent over parabolic molds, shaped laboriously by beating with mallets and hammers, and tested with brass gauges. When completed, with a burner in the focus, measurements were taken of the intensity of the light at various points of the reflected beam.[29] Some of these reflectors were reported to have been used for thirty-eight years with no perceptible harm from cleaning. Again, Lewis's reflectors did not measure up; far from being parabolic in shape, they were shaped more like wash basins; the thin metal was easily bent in cleaning, and the silvered reflecting surface was so thin that it was soon scrubbed off by keepers lacking proper cleaning supplies.[30]

Criticism of Lewis's lights mounted, and Lewis in turn blamed the keepers. In 1817, he wrote, "How much the alteration has added to the brilliancy of the lights must depend on the keepers. Boston Light, which, with the old lamps could not be seen over 5 or 6 leagues, can now be seen 9 or 12 leagues; all the lights having

Fig. 18. Manufacture of parabolic reflector. Stevenson, *A Rudimentary Treatise*.

been fitted on the same principle, the improvement would be equally great in all, were they all equally well attended."[31]

As Lewis installed the lamps, moreover, he compounded the growing problem of confusing lights with one another, for he sometimes took it on himself to change established characteristics. The Boston light, which had been a fixed light for nearly a century, he made revolving, no doubt because it would appear brighter than if stationary. When subsequently he fitted the Cape Cod light with his lamps and reflectors, he changed that one from revolving to fixed, probably to distinguish it from the light at Boston. In European countries, as we have seen, when such changes were to be made or new lights added, the practice was to notify mariners with published announcements months in advance and to distribute this information to foreign vessels. This procedure was not followed in the United States, sometimes with dire consequences. In 1816, for instance, the decaying twin light on Baker's Island was rebuilt as a single stone tower (a decision in which Lewis no doubt had a part). Previous to the change, a China trade vessel, the *Union*, had left Salem for Penang. Returning home on a February night in 1817, the captain was caught in a snowstorm and mistook the light for Boston. He ran aground, and, after a safe journey of thousands of miles, his cargo of pepper and tin, valued at $120,000, was lost off the coast of Massachusetts.[32]

The most vocal critic of the country's lights was Edmund March Blunt, publisher of nautical works. In the 1817 edition of *The American Coast Pilot*, Blunt warned sailors of a dangerous situation:

> With all deference to the opinion of those who regulate and provide for Light Houses on the Coast, we recommend the absolute necessity, that the greatest notoriety be given when any change is made in the mode of exhibiting Lights, which guide the Mariner, and on which his life often depends. We again repeat, BOSTON LIGHT HOUSE contains a REVOLVING LIGHT which will appear brilliant FORTY SECONDS and be obscured TWENTY SECONDS, alternately CAPE COD light House is erected on the Clay Pounds and contains a FIXED LIGHT; and the Light House on Race Point, contains a REVOLVING LIGHT.[33]

Blunt did not mention Lewis by name, but there is no doubt for whom his admonition was intended. In order to keep *The American Coast Pilot* up to date, Blunt was in regular contact with navigators and others with nautical interests and knew better than any the state of the lights. Blunt's outspoken criticism of the lighthouse administration was continued by his sons and eventually bore fruit in the reforms of 1852.

Perhaps in response to criticism, in 1817 Lewis published *Descriptions of the Light Houses on the Coast of the United States*. Identifying himself a "Superintendent for Lighting the United States' Light-Houses," he introduced the work by stating, "Several alterations having been made in the Light-Houses on the American Coast, and several new ones lately erected, have induced the subscriber to publish the following descriptions of them for the benefit of navigators." For each of the fifty-one lighthouses then standing, he gave the characteristic of its beacon, its height above sea level, the depth of nearby waters, and sailing directions of varying usefulness. The list descended geographically from Passamaquody in the north to St. Simon's Island in the south. *Descriptions* was surely helpful for coastal navigation, but omission of bearings of latitude or longitude limited its utility, especially for sailors arriving from the open sea. The entry for Baker's Island read,

> There were formerly two lanterns, one elevated 15 feet above the other; these have been taken down, and one Stone Tower erected, the lantern on which is elevated 70 feet above the level of the sea, and contains a fixed light. Should this or Scituate light be made in the night, in thick weather, and a doubt should arise, which, it may be ascertained by sounding; if Baker's Island Light, there will be 40 to 50 fathoms water; if Scituate Light, there will be 15 to 22 fathoms.[34]

Fig. 19. Stephen Pleasonton, who served as Superintendent of U.S. lighthouses from 1820 to 1852. Courtesy of the Smithsonian Institution.

In 1820, Stephen Pleasonton was appointed fifth auditor of the Treasury in charge of navigational aids. For the first time, a single individual was solely in charge of lighthouses, with no other duties to distract him; but, as it turned out, the only improvement was prompter payment of bills. Pleasonton was proud of his "economies," boasting often that he spent less than Congress appropriated on construction and lighting. Though the number of lights grew rapidly, along with the contractors, collectors, and keepers that serviced them, Pleasonton held no one accountable for performance. He considered himself a fiscal agent and for advice on nautical matters turned to Winslow Lewis.

But, even as Lewis exerted new influence through Pleasonton, his own role was changing. Though his contract for delivering oil was renewed in 1822 for five more years, thereafter he lost out in this work[35] By 1827, enough objection had been raised to his lucrative monopoly that Pleasonton put a contract out to bid for delivery of oil and lighthouse repairs. New Bedford oil dealer C. Grinnell, Jr., underbid Lewis and won the contract.[36]

Thereafter, Lewis concentrated his efforts on lighthouse construction. In this area, too, he had got his start early. In 1816, when the war was over and new lights authorized, Dearborn had turned to Lewis for assistance. For lights to be erected at Point Gammon near Hyannis and Tarpaulin Cove, Dearborn asked him to select the best sites and recommend construction materials. Lewis, for his part, turned to others for help. At Point Gammon, he reported to Dearborn,

> Mr. Reed, a member of Congress from that quarter, went with the persons to fix upon the site. . . . He says there are plenty of fine building stones on the land and I therefore recommend a round stone light House built with split, undressed stone, 20 feet high, diameter of the base 16 feet, diameter of the top 8 feet, Lantern 6 feet in diameter and seven feet hight. . . . I think that the buildings will be as permanent and durable as if built of dressed stone and not near so expensive. The cost I estimate at $3,500.

For Tarpaulin Cove, Lewis recommended a building similar to that at Point Gammon, but of wood instead of stone, as the appropriation was only $2,500.

In view of these building practices—leaving the choice of sites to members of Congress and others without expertise, using local undressed stones for construction, tailoring structures to available funds—it is not surprising that repairs to towers and dwellings ran high. By the 1840s, half the annual lighthouse expenditures were spent on repairs. When Lewis found himself blamed for these problems, he again blamed the system from which he had profited so well, saying that limited appropriations were the cause of "the second class lighthouses not being built with more expensive and permanent materials."[37]

France, meanwhile, had developed a high degree of sophistication in its navigational aids, a result of establishing itself as a sea power. A Department of Phares et Balises (lighthouses and beacons) had been created within the Ministry of Public Works after the French Revolution, and in 1811 Napoleon created a Commission des Phares to encourage further improvement of navigational lighting. Appointed to the com-

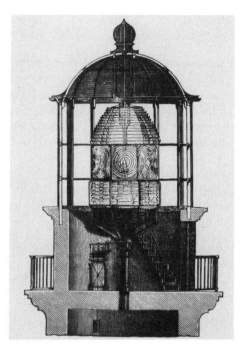

Fig. 20. An early example of a first-order Fresnel lens, composed of more than one thousand pieces of glass. Note the steps leading to the lantern room. Courtesy of the U.S. Lighthouse Society.

mission were prominent scientists and military men who understood that good coastal lighting was vital to commerce and defense.[38]

This organization was the structure for development of the Fresnel (pronounced fre-NEL) lens that would revolutionize navigational lighting. Young Augustin Fresnel (1788–1828) was appointed to the commission in 1819, soon after winning an award from the Académie des Sciences for a paper on diffraction of light. He had proposed that light was transmitted in waves and not the discrete particles hypothesized by Newton, a theory that had shaped physics for more than a century. Fresnel's experiments with refraction, using prisms to bend light rays into narrow beams, showed this method far more effective than reflection in capturing light from a flame. His appointment to the commission allowed him to construct the first successful lighthouse lens, by arranging sets of prisms around a single lamp.

Fig. 21. Augustin Fresnel (1788–1828), whose invention of the Fresnel lens in 1823 revolutionized the science of lighthouse optics. Courtesy of the Smithsonian Institution.

It was first displayed at France's Cordouan lighthouse in 1823 and produced a beam of light four times stronger than any produced by reflectors. Alan Stevenson, Robert's son, wrote of Fresnel's achievement, "I know of no work of art more beautifully creditable to the boldness, ardor, intelligence, and zeal of the artist."[39]

Alan Stevenson visited Corduouan to see the lens for himself and in 1824 went to Paris to meet Augustin and his brother, Léonor. Stevenson, who with other members of his family had brought reflector lighting near perfection, was excited about the possibilities of this new system. He brought a lens, lamp, and revolving mechanism to Edinburgh, where he used it for his own experiments at the Inchkeith light.

During these early years of the nineteenth century, lighthouse boards of several European countries, but especially Great Britain and France, worked out solutions to problems that afflicted navigational lighting. As the number of lights increased, for instance, various systems evolved for distinguishing one from another. In Great Britain, different strengths (determined by the number of lamps) of reflector lights were used for landfall, coastal, and harbor lights. Red glass was occasionally added for further distinctions. Meanwhile, the clockwork mechanism operating revolving lights became more precise, and new flashing patterns for identification came into use.[40] In France, a somewhat different system evolved. When Fresnel created his famous lens, he developed several strengths of light, or orders, by increasing the number of concentric lamp wicks in the single, central lamp.* Huge first-order lenses were assigned to prominent headlands and decreasing orders, down to the sixth, to lesser sites. Colored glass was not used as it would reduce the efficacy of these distinctions. In 1825, another member of the French commission, Rear Admiral Roussel, proposed a further improvement, the distribution of lights along a coast in a regular sequence of patterns, spaced so that one would always be in view. Since a strong light was visible twenty-one nautical miles in clear weather from the deck of a ship, first-order lenses were installed approximately every forty-two miles on points of land visible from the open sea and lights of lesser orders spaced between them.

The French commission and the various boards of Great Britain took care that fuel was of the first quality before distributing it to the lighthouses. Because of the great variability in the quality of whale oil, it was tested by burning quantities from each lot for several hours to determine cleanliness and combustibility. As the price of whale oil increased, however, France experimented with alternatives and eventually substituted colza oil pressed from the seed of wild cabbage. Not only was colza cheaper, but it burned more cleanly and at lower temperatures than whale oil and did not char the wicks so quickly. Eventually, Trinity House also adopted colza for use in English lighthouses.

Lantern design was a further source of difficulty in early lighthouses, for the thick wrought-iron framework and small panes of glass obstructed passage of the light; moreover, poor ventilation caused soot and moisture to be deposited inside, obscuring the glass and eroding the supports. During the first half of the nineteenth century, stronger metals such as cast iron and bronze came into use, making possible the use of larger panes of glass. By mid-century, diagonal rather than vertical bracing

---

*The order of a Fresnel lens refers to its focal distance, i.e., the distance from the light source to the inner surface of the lens. The focal distance of a first-order lens is 36.2 inches, while that of a sixth-order lens is only 5.9 inches.

was used in the best lanterns, allowing even more light to pass through and providing greater stability in high winds.[41] Meanwhile, an Englishman, Professor Farraday, developed an ingenious solution for improved ventilation by fitting copper tubes over the glass lamp chimneys through which the products of combustion escaped to the outside. These tubes also produced a steadier flame, reducing breakage of the glass chimneys. By the mid-nineteenth century, ventilator tubes were commonly used in Europe wherever reflector lamps were employed.

Fresnel served as secretary/engineer with the Commission des Phares until his death from tuberculosis at the tragically early age of 37. Alan Stevenson praised him as "classed with the greatest of those inventors who extend the boundaries of human knowledge; . . . wherever maritime intercourse prevails, the solid advantages which his labors have produced will be felt and acknowledged."[42] Fresnel himself was a modest man. Of the honors that came to him he wrote, "All the compliments I have received . . . never gave me so much pleasure as the discovery of a theoretic truth, or the confirmation of a calculation by experiment."[43] After his death, his brother, Léonor, filled his position on the commission and took as his mission the education of foreign governments interested in the use of the Fresnel lens.

Holland was the first foreign nation to adopt the Fresnel lens system. Soon after, in 1834, the commissioners of the northern lights asked Alan Stevenson to determine if it should be adopted in Scotland, replacing the reflector system developed by the Stevenson family. After careful study and consultation with Léonor, Alan concluded decisively in favor of lenses.[44] Soon after, he was employed by Trinity House to superintend construction of the first English example of a first-order lens, at Start Point in Devonshire. By 1852, when the new U.S. Light House Service ordered Fresnel lenses installed in all American lighthouses, they already marked the coasts of Ireland, Belgium, Denmark, Norway, Sweden, Russia, Italy, Spain, Portugal, Egypt, Turkey, and Brazil.[45]

In the United States, meanwhile, Lewis and other contractors continued to dominate expansion of the lighthouse system. Growing criticism led fifth auditor Pleasonton to introduce some changes, such as improved lanterns, larger reflectors of twenty-one inches in diameter, and gradual removal of the thick glass in front of Lewis's original apparatus; but the unfortunate policy of awarding contracts to the lowest bidder assured work of inferior quality. (Lewis wrote many of the contract specifications, and, not surprisingly, was often the winning bidder. In 1843, he claimed to have built nearly one hundred lighthouses in the United States.) Other questionable practices continued. Because revolving mechanisms were so crude, characteristics of new lights continued to be created through establishment of double and even triple towers.[46] Moreover, the number of lamps in a light bore little relation to its importance for navigation; in 1842, for instance, Scituate Harbor light had fifteen lamps to serve local traffic, while important lights at Boston and Monomoy Point had only fourteen and eight, respectively.[47]

In 1842, the House Committee of Commerce conducted a hearing into proposed changes to the lighthouse administration, but Whig supporters of Lewis and Pleasonton controlled the proceedings and little was done. Pleasonton stated without fear of challenge, "I have never had, and do not wish to have, an engineer, or other attaché, employed by the year, at a heavy expense." The committee concluded, "Every innovation is not an improvement. When an old and well-tried system works tolerably well, change and experiments should be avoided. More time and further experience will furnish correctives far better than any which may be anticipated from a change of system and a displacement of those who have thus far given that system a claim upon the confidence of the country."[48] And so things continued for nine more years.

4

David Melville and the Gas Lights

By the time Winslow Lewis entered the lighthouse business, whale oil had replaced inferior oils such as fish and seal oil as a lamp fuel. Yet, even while the monopoly of the whale fishery seemed secure, a surprising alternative was proposed by a citizen of Newport, David Melville. Born in 1773 and a contemporary of Lewis's, Melville spent most of his life in Newport, left a provincial backwater following destruction by the British during the Revolution.[1] A pewter maker like his father, Melville also owned a hard-goods store and, as a further source of income, operated a public bathhouse with twenty "apartments" in the first floor of his house on the corner of Pelham and Thames streets.[2]

Around the turn of the century, Melville learned of European attempts to distill hydrogen gas from coal for use as an illuminant. Experimenters in England and Germany had some small successes in the late eighteenth century, but the first practical production of gas is credited to the English engineer William Murdoch, who in 1792 used gas to light his house in Cornwall and in 1802 installed gas light and heat in the engine works of Boulton, Watt and Company near Birmingham. By 1805, gas fueled one thousand burners in the cotton mills of Manchester. Word of these triumphs spread quickly. Though the details of manufacture were held secret, Americans soon were trying their own experiments, Melville among them.[3]

Fig. 22. David Melville (1773–1856), pioneer in the manufacture of flammable gas. For one year, 1817–18, he illuminated the lighthouse at Beavertail with this cleaner, brighter fuel. Courtesy of Raymond Goddard and the Smithsonian Institution.

In 1806, Melville lit a gas lamp on the porch of his house on Pelham Street. This may have been the first public display of gas light in the States.[4] He continued to refine his process and took out a patent in 1810. Three years later, he took out a second patent, stating that the improved gas lamps could light "manufactories, mines, mills, streets, theatres, light-houses, and other buildings."[5] Melville hoped to manufacture the apparatus himself, but he needed a backer. He found one in no other than Winslow Lewis, who in January 1813 loaned him $2,000.[6]

Melville was now ready to go public. He constructed a larger apparatus in his basement and announced in the *Newport Mercury* that his bathhouse would be lighted with gas lamps and the public admitted for a fee of twenty-five cents.[7] He had, he claimed, produced "Hydrogenous Gas or inflammable air . . . by the chemical process on Pit-Coal in a much more agreeable and less expensive manner than has hitherto been done by any other method." The apparatus was so simple, he continued, that "any person of ordinary faculties" could be taught to operate it in one day. Indeed, the gas lamps were much less troublesome than trimming and tending oil lamps.[8]

Crowds flocked to his house and public baths to admire the lights and learn about the process, information that Melville freely shared. Word of his success spread, and factories began to place orders, including the Seth Bemis Manufacturing Company, of which Lewis was part owner, and the Wenscott Manufacturing Company near Providence.

With success, however, came problems. Commercial production proved more expensive than Melville had anticipated, and he had to raise the cost per lamp from $10 to $13, a price that discouraged his customers. A factory owner in Patterson, New Jersey, wrote that the cotton business was booming there and that, though he wished to use gas lighting, he could not afford to install it. Melville also had difficulty filling small orders in distant places. Business flagged, and, to make matters worse, Lewis wrote that he was reluctant to invest more until he saw greater prospect of success.

Perhaps this crisis is what led to a new business arrangement, with Lewis as the principal partner. The Arkwright cotton mill in Providence, for instance, soon contracted directly with Lewis for an apparatus "in every respect similar to that in use in Newport." The lighting was to be installed by Melville, however, and it was he who acted as operation and safety adviser. But, despite Melville's precautions, one night a watchman entered the gashouse with a lighted candle, and the ensuing explosion caused his death and destroyed the building.[9] Incidents such as this one hurt Melville's enterprise, while gas production elsewhere was enjoying commercial success. In 1816, Baltimore became the first city to establish a public gasworks.[10]

Melville continued to hope, however, that gas would prove useful in lighthouses. In 1811, he had written to Christopher Champlin, an acquaintance in Washington, that he had heard a rumor that the government contemplated using gas as a fuel in lighthouses. He hoped, he continued, that the idea arose from such a suggestion in his patent and asked Champlin to inquire if the government might adopt his plan if he could prove by experiment that gas was superior to whale oil and at half the cost.[11] Melville particularly hoped to conduct a trial at the Newport light at Beavertail, where he could oversee operations closely. Moreover, William Ellery, Newport's now ancient collector of customs, was a friend and supporter. In 1816, Ellery appointed Melville's father-in-law, Captain George Shearman, as keeper of the lighthouse.

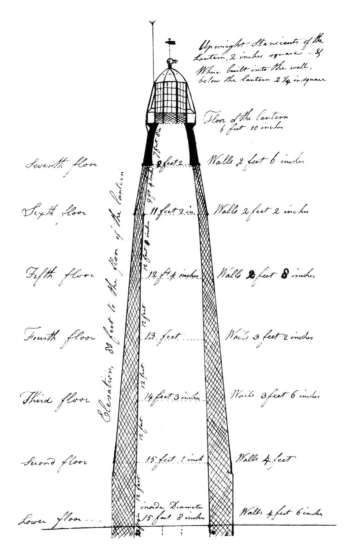

Fig. 23. Cross section of Beavertail Lighthouse drawn by David Melville. Courtesy of the National Archives New England Region.

In 1817, Melville finally won his chance. In a contract dated 27 May, the Treasury Department agreed to allow Melville to light the Newport light with gas for a period of one year. Melville agreed to furnish a complete apparatus with gasometers and pipes of copper, to build a stone gas house, to furnish all the raw materials needed to produce the light, and to give his "personal attendance."[12] But, shortly before, Lewis had begun his seven-year contract to deliver whale oil to the lights. His cooperation had to be secured, and he agreed to suspend delivery to Beavertail during the trial period: "To aid anything where there is a possibility of benefiting the public I am at all times willing to make some sacrifice, and do now agree to relinquish my contract with the commissioner of the Revenue for supplying the United States Light House on Beavertail near Newport for one year from the first day of June next and no longer."[13]

The *Newport Mercury* announced the upcoming trial, asking mariners to take special notice:

> Arrangements have . . . been made for determining whether Gas may not be advantageously substituted for oil in the lighthouses of the United States. The experiment is to be made in the lighthouse in Newport, Rhode Island. It is particularly recomended to the attention of mariners, from whom communications . . . as to its relative benefits or inconvenience when compared with oil are invited.

The same article noted that four new lights would be built that summer in Massachusetts, the first since the war had ended.[14] A new era in lighthouse construction was beginning, and with it came the promise of huge profits for whomever supplied the fuel.

To produce gas for lighthouse use, coal or some other carbon product was placed in a small oven, or retort, and sealed with a lute of clay and sand. A fire was built, driving out hydrogen gas and leaving behind a residue. The gas passed through condensers in the cistern to be purified and then was stored in gasometers inverted in the cistern. Each gasometer was hung on a pulley and balanced with weights. When gas was needed, weights were removed and the gasometer dropped, forcing gas through the pipes to the burners. Each burner had its own key, or valve, and all were controlled by a valve in the main tube.[15]

The large cisterns inside the gashouse were made of planks lined with lead. Melville and Ellery had discussed using salt water to purify the gas, but, considering

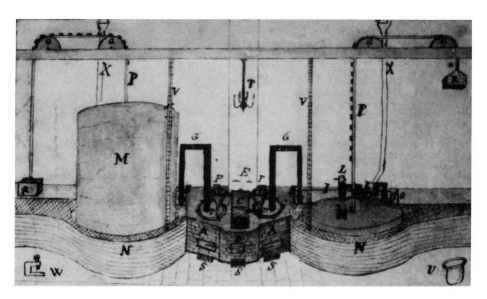

Fig. 24. Diagram of a gas-making apparatus from David Melville's Meteorological Table and Diary, ca. 1817. Courtesy of Newport Historical Society.

that the salt would be "extremely destructable" to the copper tubing, they decided on fresh. Melville sank a well nearby—which must have pleased the keeper, who had previously had to go a "great distance" for his water.[16] The gasometers, five feet in diameter and nine feet high, had a capacity of sixteen hundred gallons each and were sealed by the water in the cistern. The cisterns initially were filled from the well; thereafter, Melville noted, rain was found sufficient for keeping the tanks filled and preventing them from stagnating.

Melville kept a careful record of the experiment in his "Meteorological Table and Diary," noting the hours the lamps were lit, the quantity of materials used and gas consumed, daily weather conditions, and any unusual occurrence. Construction was completed on 8 October, and over the next several days Melville replaced the ten whale oil lamps with an equal number of gas burners and instructed the keeper in their operation. On 23 October, when all were installed, the deputy collector, Captain Cahoone, came to inspect. He reported that the flame of the gas lights was brighter and more intense than the whale oil lamps, using scientific criteria of that

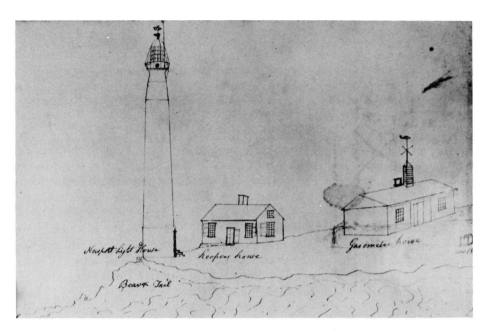

Fig. 25. Sketch of Beavertail Lighthouse and gashouse, frontispiece of David Melville's Meteorological Table and Diary, ca. 1817. Courtesy of Newport Historical Society.

time: "When the [whale oil] lamps were lit and . . . put in the best order and filled with the best oil, no shadow could be seen to fall from the body at one or two hundred yards distance. With the gas lights at the same distance, the shadow of the body at the ground is as strong as from the moon the 8th and 10th day."[17]

On 17 November, Melville was informed by a John Gorton from Block Island that the light was visible there in clear weather. He "observed [it] to be much better than formerly, did not know the cause—thought a New Lantern had been put on the Light House." On 18 November, Winslow Lewis visited the lighthouse, examined the gas apparatus, and, as Melville wrote at the time, "seemed much pleased with it." But this was not the whole truth, as we shall see.

Not only did the gas lights please mariners, but they did much to ease the keeper's lot as well. Though with gas light the keeper still had to climb the seventy-eight-foot tower at dusk and dawn to ignite and extinguish the burners, he no longer had to carry endless buckets of whale oil with him. The gas was emitted directly from the burners, so he no longer had to trim charred wicks in the middle of the night. And, since the gas burned cleanly, he no longer had to wipe soot from the windows, glass chimneys, and reflectors. Operation was so simple, in fact, that within a few weeks Melville could report that the keeper's fourteen-year-old assistant "makes the gas, cleans and lutes the retorts, and manages the apparatus as well as could be wished, lights up and regulates the flame and appears to understand every part of the operation perfectly well."[18]

During the first months of the undertaking, Melville experimented with methods of gas production. At first, he used pine tar instead of coal as his raw material and heated the retort in which it was sealed with a mixture of charcoal and Rhode Island coal.[19] In early December, one of the retorts cracked. After installing a new one, Melville made adjustments to lessen the heat.[20] Eventually, he substituted pine wood for coal, finding "the heat more uniform and less destructive to the retorts." Experimenting further, he added rosin to the tar and discovered it burned with a whiter flame, consumed less gas, and reduced the time of production almost by half.[21] For a while, he added spirits of tar to liquify the rosin and tar mixture, but, when he realized it gave a blue root to the flame, he stopped.

In late January, the size of the flames suddenly decreased. Melville reinstalled five whale oil lamps and found ice on the main valve in the lantern room. Heat from the furnace had raised steam from the cisterns, which then passed through the tubing along with the gas, causing the ice to form. To prevent a recurrence, Melville added a small burner to warm the main valve. But on 2 February the gas stopped again. This time, it turned out, ice had blocked the main tube. Melville explained why: "The pipe was intended to be laid in the earth below the reach of frost, but it was found impractical to get a passage through the foundation of the lighthouse, and we were under the necessity of bringing it above ground to convey it through the wall. To prevent frost it was cased up and covered with seaweed, but it was not beyond the reach of the late severe frost." He added more seaweed and drew gas only from the fuller of the gasometers, which had less water vapor. The freezing did not occur again.[22]

The lights operated without difficulty for several months. But one August morning Melville found them out altogether and discovered that the main valve had been turned off during the night. At the time, the keeper's house was being rebuilt, and Melville suspected the mason's boys, who were lodged in the lighthouse, to be the culprits: "Obliged them to quit the lighthouse, and find other lodgings, in consiquence [*sic*] of making cigars in the light house, and carelessness with their lamp, indangering [*sic*] its safety."[23]

Melville was eager to make further improvements at Beavertail. The previous spring, Ellery had asked Melville if he thought that frost would continue to collect on the inside of the windows in winter, as it did when oil lamps were used. Melville guessed that it would not, he told Ellery, because a stove would no longer be needed to warm the lantern room to keep the oil fluid, and he believed that this was the source of the moisture.[24] Nonetheless, by late October Melville observed humidity collecting on the window and obscuring the light for one or two hours after lighting: "The keeper informs me it is common in some states of the air, at this season particularly."[25] Melville was puzzled by the phenomenon and noted in his diary whenever the Point Judith light, only nine miles away, was invisible, supposing it to be obscured for the same reason. When colder weather caused frost to form, the problem became acute. Melville experimented with air flow in the lantern room and on 25 December wrote exultantly:

> After a variety of experiments have discovered a method to prevent the collection of humidity and frost on the windows and the lanterns. I now find by keeping the Air ports in the lantern open, so that the temperature of the internal air is nearly upon an equilibrium with the external air and keeping the scuttle closed to exclude the vapor from passing up from below, no humidity or frost will collect.[26]

Melville reported that several mariners told him that the light was visible at much greater distances than previously. But the fair-minded Melville also noted that

> mariners who arrive in this harbour and compare it with Point Judith light generally think this not so good as that—though some have thought and reported to the contrary. It ought to be considered, that this is a fixed light, and shows no more than three lights reflected in any direction, while Point Judith is a revolving light, and shows ten lights reflected in every direction, at every revolution and that *that* is fitted with lens, and this is not.*

---

*It is notable that Melville accepted the conventional wisdom that the lens on Lewis's apparatus added to the strength of the light.

Despite the success of the experiment, all was not well behind the scenes. In December 1817, William Ellery reported sinister happenings to the commissioner of the revenue, Stephen Smith:

> There is good reason to believe, those who are concerned in the Whale fishery are making every effort to prevent the Gas Lights from going into operation. . . . The Keeper . . . has been questioned by a person from Nantucket on Sundry points relative to the expense of the apparatus and materials, & the management and application of the Gas. It was distinctly stated to him that they were determined on the destruction of the apparatus. . . . [T]hey were determined to destroy it, by offering a contract to furnish the United States with oil upon such advantageous terms, that Gas could not stand in competition with it, and thus they would make a sacrifice of 10,000 dollars to defeat the plan of lighting with Gas.[27]

To save themselves this trouble, Ellery continued, the Nantucketers had proposed to Melville that they would pay him the $10,000 directly for his experiment to fail. Ellery had no doubt about Melville's response: "I cannot believe that he ever will disgrace himself, and dishonor those who have favored him with their patronage."[28] Melville, as we shall see, was later to shed considerably more light on this disagreeable episode.

For now, however, it was clear only that the opposition of the whale oil dealers continued to make life difficult for Melville, as is evident from the end of his diary, where he wrote, "Considering the arduousness of the undertaking on my part, the prejudices I have had to combat, the obstacles that have been thrown in the way, . . . it has succeeded beyond my most sanguine expectations." Despite favorable comments by individual mariners, his efforts to attract influential supporters were ignored. It is easy to understand why this was so. Melville was an outsider to the fraternity of mariners. Most nautical men, and many tradesmen on land as well, were connected with the whale fishery and had much to lose if Melville were successful.

Despite this indifference—and worse—Melville was still hopeful at the year's conclusion of his experiment that the undertaking would continue. In his last entry, for 23 October 1818, he stated proudly, "That nothing has occurred to injure the reputation of the Gas Lights.. . . . I bow with reverential awe, in thankfulness to that Omnipotent Being, who formed the universe out of chaos and who said 'Let there be light,' and there was light." He sent his accounts and a copy of his diary to the secretary of the Treasury. In the course of the year, he had used thirty-eight barrels of tar, five barrels of rosin, five hundred bushels of charcoal, twelve bushels of Rhode Island coal, and eleven and one-quarter cords of pine wood and produced 347,935 gallons of hydrogen gas.[29] He was pleased to hear back shortly that the government was satisfied that he had fulfilled his contract faithfully. At the secretary's request, Boston's collector of customs Henry A. S. Dearborn traveled down to assess the experiment and gather opinions of those who had seen the light. Melville gave him a demonstration at the lighthouse, and Dearborn was impressed. He reported that it was the best light that could be produced and that the money it saved would pay for the cost of the fixtures and the salary of someone to operate it, and he recommended that gas lighting be adopted at lighthouses wherever it could be conveniently introduced.[30]

But Melville's hopes were soon dashed. Thirty-six years later, he described the sad end of his experiment:

> A letter was received from the Secretary of the Treasury. . . . He had seen my Diary . . . and was much pleased with the particular observations and remarks it contained. . . . But owing to the opposition to the use of Gas in the Light Houses by those engaged in the Whale-fishery, and the dealers in Whale Oil generally, and the existing contract to furnish the Light Houses with Oil for five years, having some time to run, Gas could not at present be adopted by the United States in the Lighthouses as a substitute; and it was considered to be the duty of the Government to encourage the Whale fishery as a Nursery for Seamen for the Navy . . . and that, in case of war and oil could not be obtained. . . , Gas could be substituted in its place . . . and in case of that event the successful experiment with gas would not be forgotten.[31]

But it was forgotten. Melville dismantled his apparatus, sold off his materials, and gave up on gas manufacture.

In 1819, the year after the Newport experiment, Melville took Lewis to court, claiming that Lewis had stolen his design for a warming lamp that would make it easier to ignite whale oil burners in cold weather. When Melville was unable to win his case for patent infringement, he apparently decided that the time had come to lay bare his version of past relations with Lewis. As recounted by Melville in *An Expose of Facts*, the story began on a November evening in 1816 when Lewis stopped by for dinner:

> Conversation turned on the difficulty of keeping lamps burning in lighthouses in very cold weather. Capt. Lewis observed he'd had many complaints of

Fig. 26. Sketch of a warming lamp patented by Winslow Lewis, 23 January 1818.

lamps going out owing to the chilling of the oil. Capt. Shearman [keeper of Beavertail and Melville's father-in-law] noted he frequently found 3 or 4 lamps out in the morning and one night last winter found 4 out at 12 p.m. and carried into the lantern a basket of wood and charcoal, and remained there till daylight putting fuel into the stove as fast as it would consume, but could not get the lamps that had gone out warm enough to light up again.[32]

Lewis responded, "You must have a larger stove in the lantern, there is no other remedy and I will send you one." Melville, however, mentioned that for several years he had known a method for keeping oil warm in Argand lamps. Because he hoped to introduce gas to the lighthouses, he had been wary of giving out the details to Lewis, for fear that he would use it with whale oil lamps and weaken the case for gas.[33] That evening, however, Lewis induced him to make a fuller sketch, and Melville informed him that should gas lights not be given a trial he intended to take out a patent for the invention.[34] Lewis replied that in a few weeks he would be in

Washington and proposed that while there he ask the commissioner of the revenue that Melville be allowed to make an experiment with gas. The experiment would be successful, he had no doubt, and would thus eliminate the need for any further improvement to the whale oil lamps. He also observed, Melville later recalled, that, under the existing law, patents were useless because so easily evaded.

As it turned out, Melville was appointed to carry to Washington the electoral votes from Rhode Island, so the following month he went there himself. He was resolved, he later stated, "to make the proposal myself to have the experiment made . . . immediately, if it could be done, if not when Lewis's contract [for delivering whale oil] had expired." While in Washington, he ran into Lewis, who promised that he would endorse the project to the commissioner of the revenue and consented to relinquish his contract for one lighthouse for one year. Later, Melville discovered that Lewis had done nothing of the sort, but by then Melville had won his contract anyway. But Lewis, in order to establish with the government that he was not opposed to the gas lights, "offered to be one of my bondsmen . . . and was actually one of them."[35]

In January 1817, after returning home, Melville made a model of his warming device and "found it to succeed so well that summer strained oil [which cost less but also ignited less easily in cold weather than winter strained oil] might be burned in the coldest weather in the most exposed situations without difficulty." In March, not yet having heard from Washington about his gas light proposal, he took steps to apply for a patent. But, when he was notified that he could proceed with his gas experiment, he postponed further work on the other.[36]

The year of the Beavertail experiment, as Melville's *An Expose of Facts* was to reveal, gave Melville cause to be increasingly wary of Lewis. Far from being pleased with the lights when he first visited the refitted Beavertail, Lewis had on the contrary told Melville flatly that he would not relinquish his contract, worth $35,000, to supply whale oil to the lighthouses, and he further stated his opinion that the government would not adopt gas lighting more widely. Later that day, back in Newport, Melville was approached by William Simons, a friend of Lewis's, who delivered the following message: "Capt. Lewis . . . thinks you had better make the best bargain you can with the Nantucket people, and produce a failure in the experiment; Capt. Lewis says he has no doubt you may obtain ten thousand dollars from them." Melville was astonished at the proposed bribe and replied to Simons that he hoped "Capt. Lewis would not mention the infamous thing to me."[37] One can only assume that Melville did not mention the bribe in his diary, but rather stated that Lewis was pleased with the experiment, because he feared that challenging the powerful Lewis publicly would jeopardize his Beavertail contract.

Melville, as we have seen, was given ample evidence that the government was unlikely to adopt gas more widely as a lighthouse fuel. At this time, he decided to pursue other projects and to seek patents for his warming device and for his discovery about how to prevent humidity and frost from collecting on lantern windows.[38] He proposed a joint venture to Lewis, presumably realizing by now that Lewis was less than scrupulous, but at the same time recognizing that lighthouse proposals without his endorsement had little chance of realization. The full extent of Lewis's duplicity was about to become known. When Melville wrote, "You . . . have the power of turning these improvements to great advantage, and I have no objection if you will promote the introduction of them, . . . making the advantages which may be derived a joint concern," Lewis replied that he had never heard of these ideas and informed Melville that other patents had already been taken out for the warming device. Melville then discovered that two patents had been taken out, one by Lewis and identical to the sketch Melville had given him. Melville, as we have seen, took the dispute to court but was unable to win his case for patent infringement. He settled for Lewis's agreement to vacate his patent and had the last word in his convincingly damning *Expose of Facts*.[39]

For some years, both men did contract work for the repair and fitting up of lighthouses, and, satisfyingly enough, Melville underbid Lewis on at least one occasion. In 1823, Melville built a lighthouse on Newport's Goat Island. A description of the lighthouse fifteen years later does little for Melville's reputation as a craftsman. In 1838, a naval officer, Lieutenant George M. Bache, reported of the twenty-foot tower, "It is at present in a very bad condition, owing to its faulty construction. . . . In consequence of deficient ventilation and the dampness of the tower, the lantern is subject to the condensation of moisture upon the inner surface of the glass, and ice is occasionally formed. I observed this condensation at the period of my visit, although the weather was moderately warm."[40] So much for Melville's improvements! The light was discontinued shortly after, not because of its condition (which was no worse than many), but because of a new light built nearby. Melville's tower had been erected on the northern end of the island, but boats sometimes ran aground at night on a reef extending beyond it. In 1838, in a foray into lighthouse matters rare for that time, the Bureau of Engineers built a dike over the reef and a granite lighthouse at the end, the one still active today.

Melville's lighthouse remained unlit for many years. In 1853, a light was authorized for Prudence Island's Sandy Point, and the unused structure was dismantled, moved, and reassembled at the new site. This now-sturdy structure is an active light today, and over its door are engraved the words "David Melville 1823."

In 1826, Melville won contracts for fitting up new lights on Dutch Island and at Warwick Neck, both in Rhode Island.[41] His involvement with Beavertail continued as well. In 1827, he beat out Lewis with a low bid for repairs to the tower and won a second contract to erect a new iron lantern.[42] A year later, he installed a six-hundred-pound bell at Beavertail atop a fifteen-foot brick tower, although the bell was removed four years later; its ring was audible only at short distances and was often drowned out by the surf.

Melville lived to a ripe old age. He was eighty years old in 1853 when Newport built its first public gasworks, his own efforts long forgotten. The *Newport Mercury*, however, ran a background story on gas manufacture and from the mechanics who in 1813 had made Melville's apparatus on Pelham Street learned of Melville's early experiments.[43] The *Mercury* subsequently published a summary based on Melville's own account and credited him with being the first to prepare gas for consumption in the United States.

In addition to this belated recognition, Melville must also have taken satisfaction in the *Report . . . of the Lighthouse Board* issued the previous year. While this lengthy condemnation of the lighthouse administration did not mention Winslow Lewis by name, he was clearly implicated as the best-known practitioner of the too often corrupt contract system. (Lewis was spared the humiliation of the *Report*, having died in 1850.)

Melville died 3 September 1856. When the new Beavertail Lighthouse was completed soon after, it employed a Fresnel lens from France instead of lamps and reflectors. It was still fueled, however, by whale oil.

Could gas have challenged whale oil as a lighthouse fuel? Probably not. Other attempts to use gas in lighthouses amounted to little. D. Alan Stevenson believed that the first use of gas was in 1818 at Salvore Lighthouse near Trieste. Though acclaimed as a "wonderful enterprise," six years later it was discontinued due to high costs and undependability.[44] Other early efforts led to nothing, defeated by the expense of transporting coal, or by difficulties of production, or, occasionally, by explosion.

One instance of gas lighting, oddly similar to Melville's experiment, for a time seemed more promising. In 1844, another devotee of gas, Benjamin F. Coston, U.S.N., introduced it as a fuel at Christiana Creek Lighthouse near Wilmington,

Delaware. Coston unwittingly claimed that the "Christiana light-house is the *first* and *only* light-house ever successfully lighted by means of gas generated in the light-house." The price of whale oil had been rising (between 1840 and 1846 it nearly doubled to $1.07 per gallon), and Coston stated that gas, installed in all the light-houses, would save the government $100,000 annually. Pleasonton was predictably unenthusiastic. As an argument against its use he cited a gas explosion at a lighthouse in England ten years earlier and urged extreme caution in making changes to the system of lighting.[45]

For a time Coston prevailed. In 1851, Pleasonton informed the board investigating lighthouses that gas was used at four sites in Delaware Bay, including Christiana Creek. Whale oil was often substituted, however, because keepers maintained the gas apparatus poorly and "were averse to making and burning gas." He conceded that gas produced from rosin was "excessively cheap" but advised against its further use: "To employ scientific men to attend [gas lights], would occasion an expense out of all proportion to the benefits to be derived from them."[46] The board, however, was not swayed by Pleasonton's negative arguments. It reported that "the persons charged with the few gas-lights now existing in this country, for want of practical and theoretical knowledge, it is believed, are not competent to report results sufficiently reliable to decide so important a question." The introduction of gas into lighthouses, it continued, had long been anticipated as an important step, and it hoped that a series of experiments might lead to a decision "as to the practicability of making the attempt in the present state of knowledge, or the best and safest means of generating, conducting, and continuing it for light-house purposes."[47]

When the Light House Service began to test new fuels, however, it first experimented with colza oil, long used in the lighthouses of France. But lard proved more economical, and this replaced whale oil for a number of years until it was itself supplanted by kerosene. A few lighthouses used gas from municipal works, but even here there were problems. The Portland Lighthouse on Lake Erie, for instance, drew gas from the town plant two miles away, but, when water collected in the pipes, whale oil lamps had to be substituted.

It might well be asked why the oil dealers feared gas at all, so strong was the whale industry in the early nineteenth century. After 1815, whaling began a spectacular rise that continued for decades and brought great wealth to investors: in 1838, the sale of oil and bone in New Bedford alone totaled more than $2 million, and related business prospered as well. But the work was risky, and even in peak years 10 percent of all whaling voyages ended in loss.[48] The stakes were high, and any challenge was viewed as a threat.

For the government, whaling promised more than wealth. Well into the nineteenth century, formal naval development was neglected. Whaling voyages, however, assured a supply of experienced seamen on which the government could draw if needed. John Adams viewed whaling as a "valuable . . . Nursery of Seamen," and after independence worked for a fisheries treaty with Great Britain, believing that a strong industry would be "a source of wealth in peace and of power in war."

But time was on the side of gas. In 1850, incorporation of a gas company in New Bedford brought this cry of outrage from the city's whaling interests:

> If New Bedford cannot help herself, who will help her. . . . Gas—gas in New Bedford, the oil market of the earth! What an example to set the world! What a caving in! What a ridiculous concession to ridiculous fashion! Who will buy our commodity after this? . . . In five years we predict, she will be a bigger ruin than Carthage. The ships will all be gone, the inhabitants all dead, the whales will fresh and smart at their leisure . . . and what good we should stop to ask will your gas-lights do you then?[49]

5

Reform

Hence it follows, that the lens apparatus is far more intense than a reflector apparatus of the same size; that, with the same intensity of light, it consumes much less oil; that, in reference to original cost, repairs, and renewals, it is more economical; that it requires a less expensive lightroom, and demands much less time and trouble from the keeper.

—Sir David Brewster, quoted by the Blunts, 25 Cong., 2d sess., S. Doc. 138

Fifty-five lighthouses marked the coast of the United States when Stephen Pleasonton became fifth auditor in 1820. By 1852, 270 more lighthouses and lightships had been built under his supervision. The country was expanding, manufacture was increasing, and steam-powered vessels transported people and goods in ever greater numbers. But, as new lights were built to guide them on their way, methods of administration did not change to meet the needs of a growing system.

Edmund March Blunt, publisher of nautical works, had long advocated better lights to assist American commerce. In the preface to the twelfth, and his last, edition of *The American Coast Pilot*, he reminded his readers that in that work he had "undertaken a duty, the performance of which belongs RATHER TO THE GOVERNMENT THAN TO AN INDIVIDUAL." In the late 1820s, his sons, Edmund and George William, took over the publishing business, renamed the firm E. & G. W. Blunt, and continued to work for safer coasts. In the early 1830s, Edmund traveled to Europe, saw Fresnel lenses used in France, and determined that they should be introduced at home. On his return, he and George began campaigning for their adoption in the United States. They recruited others to the cause, including their friend Matthew Calbraith Perry, a naval officer in New York.[1]

Fig. 27. 1813 engraving of the *Chancellor Livingston*, one of the earliest passenger steamers to operate in New England. Providence Public Library.

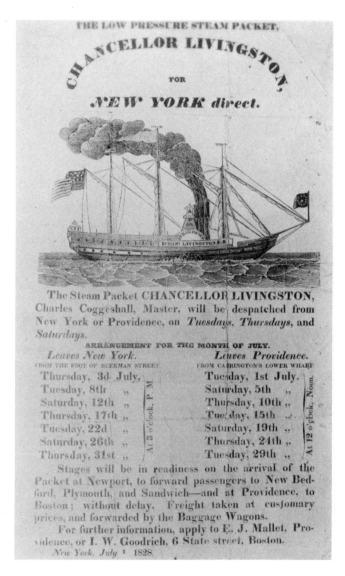

Fig. 28. Schedule of the *Chancellor Livingston*'s Providence–New York run in 1828. Providence Public Library.

In 1837, public dispute erupted between the blunts and Pleasonton. The episode began when George and Edmund wrote to the secretary of the Treasury that they believed that the lighthouse system had grown beyond the ability of one person to administer. They urged frequent examination of all aspects of operation, from construction, to optics, to the performance of the keepers. Until change was instituted, they asserted, "our light houses will remain a reproach to the great country, feebly and inefficiently managed, and at the mercy of contractors." Pleasonton, they charged, though fiscally competent, relied too much on contractors for carrying out the work of superintendence. Pleasonton responded by gathering testimonials about the lights, boasted of the economy with which he ran the system, and praised Winslow Lewis, the "contractor" to whom the Blunts obviously referred, "to whose experience and knowledge in all that relates to lighthouses, I have been indebted for the present and past good condition of the whole establishment."[2] The Blunts answered this by pointing out that Pleasonton's supporters were mostly local seamen who did not know the better lights abroad. They pointed out also that nearly one-third of the previous year's expenditures went for repairs and cited a recent wreck caused by a bad light that had cost $350,000 in insurance—considerably more than the annual expenditure on all the country's lighthouses.[3]

Perry, meanwhile, had recently inspected the navigational aids of New York harbor and wrote Pleasonton that he believed that the customs collectors could not supervise the lighthouses adequately. In New York, for instance, the collector was responsible for "a dozen lighthouses and a great many buoys, beacons, and other aids, some of them 200 miles apart." Better, he suggested, would be a board of four or five naval officers and an engineer to visit each light annually, to inspect oil and oversee all matters to do with construction and repair. As for the keepers, only retired shipmasters and mates should be appointed.[4]

Pleasonton responded that he had no objection to a board of naval officers who would reinforce the inspections of the collectors and contractors. But an engineer, he continued, would be of no value at all, "as the lighthouses are built and repaired upon information already possessed by the office, and I should therefore be opposed to uniting one, at a considerable expense, no doubt, to the proposed board." The system in general was in good order, he claimed.[5]

But there were further hints of disaffection; that same year, the Senate Committee of Commerce, chaired by a Blunt supporter, halted an appropriation of nearly $1 million for lighthouse construction. The committee amended the bill, requiring that naval officers inspect the proposed sites to determine if all were needed. Thirty-one projects were stopped, two of them in southern New England.

The officers sent to investigate a proposed light for Bristol, Rhode Island, encountered a raging dispute about the best site. Some advocated Hog Island to the north, claiming that a light on Papoose Squaw Point (today known as Poppasquash Point) would be obscured by high land on nearby Prudence Island. Others argued that Hog Island was unsuitable because of the shoal extending southward; to build a light on the shoal was prohibitively expensive, but one on the island proper might mislead the unwary. The naval officers, however, believed that neither site was as good as nearby Sandy Point on Prudence Island and recommended further study.[6]

The secretary of the Navy was alarmed by the committee report on operation of the country's lighthouses. Some proposals for new construction, it appeared, had come from those with land to sell or who hoped for a building contract or to be made lighthouse superintendent. Many existing lighthouses, on the other hand, were clearly "susceptible of improvement, either in character or position." The secretary inquired of Congress,

> When the great importance of the lighthouse system is considered, its relation
> to safety of human life, and vast amounts of property; the facilities and rapidity of communication, which it gives between the different parts of our extensive Atlantic and lake coasts, and the cost of establishing and supporting it,
> the Board would respectfully suggest whether some additional measures may
> not be desirable for obtaining the necessary information, to secure the greatest
> public advantages from expenditure which may hereafter be authorized for
> these purposes.[7]

In 1838, the Senate Commerce Committee was chaired by John Davis of Massachusetts, a friend of George Blunt's. At his instigation, the committee authorized the purchase of two Fresnel lenses and one set of lamps and reflectors from England. The reflector lights would be installed at Boston and the lenses, a first-order fixed and a second-order revolving, at Sandy Hook and Navesink lighthouses in New Jersey.[8] This was not the first time that a trial of lenses had been proposed. "Some years past," Winslow Lewis later remarked, he had received a memoir from a French naval officer on a new system of lighting. It worked by "substituting a great number of lenses, peculiarly formed, instead of the reflectors. On examining the specifications and drawings, I found it altogether too complicated, as well as too expensive, and too liable to injury to be introduced into our light-houses."[9] A further reason was surely the fact that each lens used only one lamp and a fraction of the oil consumed by Lewis's lamps and reflectors.

Matthew Calbraith Perry, in Europe on other business, undertook to make these purchases and to learn what he could about the illumination of British and French lighthouses. He concluded that the French system was superior to England's but nonetheless noted that "the brilliancy of both . . . is so remarkable, compared with the dimness of the American lights, that no one can avoid noticing the difference."[10]

Perry reported to Congress on his other findings. Keepers, for instance, were treated with strict discipline: "While in Europe, the severest penalties are inflicted upon a light-house keeper who shall absent himself even for an hour from his post, in this country it is notorious that some of our principal light-houses are left for days in charge of incompetent and irresponsible persons not recognized by the regulations of the superintendent at Washington." He was particularly impressed with the ingenuity with which certain problems were solved. Trinity House, for instance, to warn ships in foggy weather near the South Stack Lighthouse had encouraged gulls "to build their nests in fissures of the rocks near the light; care is taken not to disturb them, and . . . they fearlessly rear their young within a few feet of the buildings, and the spot being known by the pilots and fishermen as the resort of these birds, the noise which they make, more especially in bad weather, gives warning to those on board of vessels brought in unexpected proximity to this dangerous point."[11]

For fuel, Perry learned that Trinity House used the best winter-pressed spermaceti oil, purchased only after careful inspection, and that, in France, colza oil was used instead. Perry was excited about the possibility that the use of colza in the United States would lessen dependence on whaling, especially in time of war. He bought ten pounds of the seed and obtained a treatise on its cultivation, which he had translated into English. He noted that the exhausted tobacco lands of Maryland and Virginia were similar to those of France and Belgium where colza was grown successfully and hoped that these areas might also prove congenial to production.[12]

Perry arranged for shipment of the Fresnel lenses, but, despite the high hopes of the reformers waiting at home, the trip did not go well. Though scheduled to be sent in April 1839, manufacture of the lenses took longer than expected, and departure was delayed until November.[13] The vessel was then damaged in a storm, put into Bermuda for repairs, and did not arrive in New York until January. Pleasonton thereupon decided, since nothing could be done in cold weather and in order to give the lenses "a full and fair trial," to request that the French send one of their best workmen to assist with installation. The workman, however, did not arrive until the following August, almost too late, according to Pleasonton, to install the lenses that year. Worse yet, it turned out that the lantern at Sandy Hook, for which one of the lenses had been destined, was too small to hold it. Both lenses in the end were installed in the twin lights at Navesink. The final cost of the operation, much higher than expected, included a sizable charge for translation—the French workman spoke no English.[14]

During an inspection a decade later, the Navesink lenses were found neglected. The keeper knew nothing about their care, nor did anyone know how to repair the mechanical lamps or the revolving machinery. The only instructions were "a small printed work, purporting to be a translation of the instructions to the light-keepers in France." The keeper did not follow these instructions, he informed the board, because someone from the New York custom house had told him to ignore them. Despite their long neglect, however, these lights were found superior to others in the area.[15]

Meanwhile, a valuable new recruit was won to the cause of reform. After a period working as a contractor for Pleasonton, I. W. P. Lewis may have been all the more sincere in his conversion since his uncle was none other than Winslow Lewis. Isaiah William Penn—known as I.W.P.—Lewis (1808–56) was the son of Winslow's brother Isaiah, whose early death had cut short I.W.P.'s education. For a number of years, I.W.P. had followed the sea, becoming master of a merchant vessel, but by age thirty he had left this life to study civil engineering in Boston. He had a special interest in lighthouse construction, particularly the foundations.[16]

Before long, I. W. P. Lewis was working for Pleasonton, introduced no doubt by his uncle. In 1837, Pleasonton asked the younger Lewis to determine the practicality of replacing the lightship at Carysfort Reef, south Florida, with a lighthouse. After reporting in favor of the project and proposing three alternate locations, Lewis gave the additional observation that the lightship was anchored five miles within the reef and likely to mislead mariners believing it to mark the reef itself. The following winter, Pleasonton contracted with Lewis to superintend construction of a lighthouse at the Southwest Pass of the Mississippi River, replacing one undermined by the river. But problems arose when Lewis complained of poor work by the builder, hired by Pleasonton. Pleasonton disagreed with Lewis's opinion, ordering a separate investigation; when this produced a condemnation of the whole project, Lewis abandoned the work as a lost cause. The builder, however, had Pleasonton transmit the case for approval to the New Orleans collector, who accepted the work as performed and paid the builder.[17]

Despite this incident, Pleasonton offered more work to Lewis, perhaps because of his expertise in foundations. Pleasonton had received an estimate of $75,000 for repairs to lighthouses at Faulkner's Island, Saybrook, and Stonington, Connecticut, and he asked Lewis to take a look. Lewis reported that there was no need for a $50,000 granite sea wall to enclose Faulkner's Island, that at Saybrook a wooden rather than a granite pier could enclose the old sea wall at considerable savings, and that at Stonington, while the $8,500 proposed for a sea wall would not suffice, a new lighthouse could instead be erected on higher ground for only $3,000. This time, Pleasonton not only took Lewis's advice but hired him to build the new pier at Saybrook and to supervise construction of the new light at Stonington (which today still stands as the Stonington Historical Society Museum).[18]

But Pleasonton soon had new reason to regret hiring Lewis, for the latter accumulated evidence against his administration by compiling a list of lighthouses that, lacking protective foundations, had been destroyed by action of the sea. To prevent such wasteful practices, Lewis proposed that an architect or engineer be employed to examine proposed sites, design suitable structures, watch over construction, and keep an eye on contractors. Such professional oversight would, of course, threaten Winslow Lewis's livelihood, and the suggestion could not have pleased either him or Pleasonton.

Meanwhile, the younger Lewis educated himself about the construction of improved lanterns. In 1839, Pleasonton contracted with him to build a new lantern for the Boston light to receive the English reflectors sent by Perry. The following year, Lewis rebuilt the Cape Cod Lighthouse, added a cast iron lantern, made a reflector apparatus similar to the English model now installed at Boston, and fireproofed the structure throughout. He subsequently installed similar lanterns, lamps, and reflectors at the Faulkner's Island and Stonington lighthouses in Connecticut and at the Tybee beacon light in South Carolina. Lewis claimed that the reflectors were manufactured as in England, with molds and dies "in obedience to optical laws." Lewis sent an example to the fifth auditor, who did not respond, however. Pleasonton had by then finally had enough of Lewis and ceased employing him as a lighthouse contractor.[19]

In 1842, Pleasonton and Winslow Lewis had opportunity to answer I. W. P. Lewis's and others' criticisms at a hearing called by their Whig supporters in the House Commerce Committee. Pleasonton defended, for instance, the practice of selecting lighthouse sites with advice from customs collectors, retired captains, and pilots. The lights, he claimed, are often "necessarily placed in low and marshy situations, to which in time the sea gains access, and renders it necessary to remove the buildings. . . . The annual expense of protecting and securing lighthouses is always considerable." He added that he would never employ an engineer by the year, at heavy expense, when he could hire, for a modest sum, the occasional services of "men of as much practical knowledge of lighthouses and submarine works as any others in the country." Winslow Lewis, for his part, claimed that "all lighthouses are judiciously located, erected in the best manner that limited appropriations permit." He charged that his nephew and his allies had proposed that construction of the lighthouses be transferred to the Topograhical Bureau because they themselves wanted employment: "I have yet to learn why an engineer is in any way required about the lighthouses. No one has ever been employed about them, in this country or in England."[20] (Lewis, of course, had no basis for this or his other claims.)

But the reformers, too, were mobilizing. On the day that the House Commerce Committee reported on this hearing, the secretary of the Treasury appointed I. W. P. Lewis to conduct an investigation of the lighthouses of Maine, New Hampshire, and Massachusetts. The report submitted by the younger Lewis offers the closest look at lighthouse operation of that time. In the course of four months, Lewis visited seventy lighthouses, nearly one-quarter of the country's total. He accumulated substantial evidence for his conclusion that the system was badly, even corruptly, managed. The most destructive practice he identified was that of contracting work to the lowest bidder, which resulted in bad lights and shoddy construction. Lack of planning, moreover, led to waste and dangerous conditions. Of the thirty-eight Massachusetts lighthouses, for instance, eight were double lights, one was a triple, twenty-five were single fixed lights, and only five were revolving. Vineyard Sound alone had twelve lights, all fixed except for Gay Head. A sailor approaching at night could easily be confused, and failure to differentiate major coastal lights from minor harbor lights compounded the problem. Lewis calculated the number of unneeded lamps, blocked by a lantern room door or shining uselessly over the land, to be 112 in the three states he visted, costing $5,000 per year to light and maintain.

Lewis showed no mercy toward his uncle: "For many years past, the specifications describing the construction and material to be used in erecting new lighthouses have been prepared by a contractor, who, in most cases, has been the successful bidder, and has erected upwards of one hundred different establishments." This situation, he charged, prevented "any honorable man of reputation and professional skill from becoming a bidder, knowing, as he must, that such a practice effectually destroys all competition." Nearly half the annual expense for lighthouse maintenance went to repair, he pointed out, a fact acknowledged by Fifth Auditor Pleasonton himself.[21]

Lewis was unique among critics of the time in his concern for the keepers. He, too, thought nautical men best suited for the work. Retired sailors, "accustomed to watch at night, . . . [are] more likely to turn out in a driving snow storm, and find their way to the light-house to trim their lamps, because in such weather they know by experience the value of a light, while . . . the landsman keeper would be apt to . . . [remain] snug in bed." Lewis considered keepers' salaries too low to "command the services of intelligent men, such as are required to do justice to a valuable and costly apparatus, when such is intrusted to them." He drew a connection between working conditions and the careless operation of many lights. Observing that it was "no uncommon occurrance to see a light gradually disappear between three and four o'clock of the morning," he noted that the practice of assigning only one keeper to a light meant that toward morning the lamps were sometimes neglected when the wicks should have been trimmed a second time. Equally disadvantageous, he found, were the appointment and dismissal of keepers on political grounds and the practice of allowing keepers to work the often more lucrative job of harbor pilot, which meant that they left the light in the charge of their wives and children. Some keepers were "active fishermen, and still more active politicians." A more serious problem, however, and one that contributed to their often poor performance, was neglect of their basic needs:

> Many keepers are compelled to endure extreme suffering from the wretched condition of the dwellings, from the want of a good boat, or any boat whatever, and from the absence of any means of obtaining pure water on the premises. If the Government neglects to furnish keepers with what common humanity demands, it cannot be expected that this humble yet useful class of citizens should be so devoted to the discharge of their duties as if provided with homes that it would be their pride to maintain in perfect order and cleanliness.[22]

Pleasonton and Winslow Lewis were predictably outraged by the report. Pleasonton maintained he had been "grossly misrepresented." An ally, Leavitt Thaxter, the collector of customs at Edgartown, came to his aid by forcing some of the keepers whom Lewis had interviewed to retract their statements.[23] Winslow Lewis for his part printed a sixty-page refutation, *A Review of the Report of I. W. P. Lewis*. He denied complaints had ever been made about the lights by seafaring or commercial men, but only by "Mr. I. W. P. Lewis and the Messrs. Blunt, whose motives are not the public good, but office." Of his nephew, he continued, "His whole knowledge has been obtained from books; with sufficient time for experience, his studies might be made useful."[24]

Despite the airing of these matters, the time for reform had not yet come. The secretary of the Treasury submitted the report of I. W. P. Lewis to Congress, recommending that no new lighthouses be approved until an engineer was employed "whose whole time shall be devoted to the regulation of the details of the lighthouse system." But Congress adjourned without action and interest in reform waned once again.[25]

Some good did result from the controversy, however. Commented a Boston journal, "The report . . . was a severe blow to the defenders of the old system; and if the Government had possessed the proper energy and vigilance, such an array of facts could not have been passed over unnoticed. A most important benefit, however, resulted . . . for it compelled the general superintendent of lighthouses to bestir himself and get things a little more to rights." Pleasonton had new lanterns and apparatus installed in all the prominent seacoast lights as fast as they could be supplied and in many of the minor lights as well. Moreover, the public was made more aware of the situation of the lights, "and the subject has by slow degrees begun to assume that importance which so properly belongs to it."[26]

The next step toward reform occurred in 1845. The Democrats were back in power, and secretary of the Treasury R. J. Walker sent two young navy lieutenants, Thornton Jenkins and Richard Bache, to Europe to learn what they could to improve lighthouses at home. After careful research, the two submitted recommendations incorporating the best features of several foreign systems. Walker endorsed their report and requested authority to appoint a board to oversee the lights. Again, Congress failed to act, but subsequent assignment of the construction of six new lighthouses to the Corp of Engineers showed a growing appreciation of the value of professionalism.[27]

A few years later, Pleasonton published a *"List of Light-Houses, Beacons, and Floating Lights of the United States, in Operation on the 1st of July, 1848, with a Statement of Their Location, Heights, Distance at Which They Are Visible in Clear Weather, etc. etc."*[28] With criticism of his administration mounting, Pleasonton no doubt wished to appear up to date. The document lacked much pertinent information, however, and was not widely circulated among navigators. Pleasonton also continued to boast of his economies. In his annual report for 1850, he stated that, since he took office, by accepting the lowest bids for construction for the 270 lighthouses built during his administration he had saved the government $347,434. This record he compared favorably with the higher costs of the British system, and, as often before, he claimed that the lighthouses of the United States were equal to any in the world.[29]

In 1851, political changes meant that reform was finally possible. Though President Zachary Taylor was a Whig, the Democrats controlled Congress, and the secretary of the Treasury, Thomas Corwin, was a special friend of George Blunt's. In March, Congress authorized Corwin to appoint a board to inquire into every aspect of the lighthouse system and to recommend legislation for improving construction, illumination, inspection, and superintendence. The board was to be composed of two high-ranking officers of the navy, two officers from the army engineers, a civilian "of high scientific attainment," and a junior naval officer as secretary.[30]

The group set to work with a will and in seven months produced a report of 760 pages documenting the problems rampant in every area of the service. Stating that "the present system of management, superintendence, and inspection, has been productive of evils which are becoming greater, daily, and which can only be arrested by radical change," the board made fifty recommendations for new legislation. Above all, it urged adoption of the lens system of illumination. Had all the country's reflector lights been fitted with Fresnel lenses, the report stated, the savings in oil for the present year alone would have been $132,185.23. It added, however, that, for a branch of public service on which human life depended, "mere saving of money, which is by no means always true economy, should not be the only guide." The board recommended that the installation of Fresnel lenses begin with the thirty-eight most important seacoast lights, including Thacher's Island, Cape Cod, and Gay Head. (The recommendation of I. W. P. Lewis, that a lighthouse with a Fresnel lens be established at Sankaty Head, Nantucket, had been carried out in 1850 by a special act of Congress after new shoals were discovered in the vicinity.) The board refuted Pleasonton's assertion that first-order lenses were not needed on the coast of the United States:

> First order lights are, if possible, *more necessary on our coast than that of any other country*. . . . The object of a light is to warn the navigator of some hidden danger, or of his approach to land, and to guide him clear of that danger on his way, or into his destined port. It therefore becomes necessary to regulate the power and range of a light, solely with reference to these primary objects. . . . There are many points along the coast of the United States, with

dangerous shoals extending many miles from them. To guide vessels clear of these dangers, lights of the greatest power and range are indispensible.[31]

The board had much to say about lighthouse construction and recommended that no new building be erected or old one repaired except under the superintendence of the Corps of Engineers. Though Winslow Lewis was nowhere mentioned by name, the results of his work (and of other contractors) were frequent targets of the report. The majority of the many lighthouses requiring extensive repair, for instance, were in states where Lewis had worked extensively.[32] "These structures," it pronounced, "are anything *but creditable to the reputation of those who have had the charge of erecting them.*" The report deplored the past "practice of this government to abandon these works to the chance management of whosoever might undertake them for the lowest sum. . . . Our light-house establishment seems to be the sole exception to our practice of building for the future as well as for the present." In particular, the board recommended centralized production of cast iron and other materials used throughout the system and finished masonry instead of local stone. As Fresnel lenses were installed, the board urged that the heights of prominent towers be raised where needed to give a range of at least twenty nautical miles. Regarding notification of mariners, the board stated emphatically,

> It is not sufficient to publish changes in a local newspaper. They should be published, as far in advance of the proposed change as possible, in all the leading commercial newspapers, nautical periodicals. . . . and distributed at home and abroad, at the customhouses and offices of the different consulates. . . . Changes . . . should never take place with less than six months' notice.[33]

On the subject of whale oil, the board noted that no article of commerce was more easily adulterated. It objected to the custom of using both summer and winter oil, as the keepers had no sure way to know one from the other. It recommended that colza oil be used as a substitute and that a reputable scientist "of high moral and social standing" should be appointed to test all fuels and equipment that were to be used for light-house purposes.[34]

A rigid system of inspection was recommended as the means by which the new order of administration would be carried out. The coasts and Great Lakes would be divided into several districts, with an officer of the Army or Navy in charge of each, responsible for inspection of the lights, attending to the needs of the keepers, superintending small repairs, and reporting to the board on the conditions. Each district would have its own supply depot, and there would also be a central depot for the whole system.[35]

To improve the performance of the keepers, the board recommended that a manual detailing information on all aspects of their work be published and prominently displayed in each lighthouse and that the information it contained be part of a qualifying exam.[36] In practice, because appointment of keepers continued to be politically influenced, more rigorous standards were slow to take hold. The performance of keepers was nonetheless greatly improved by regular inspections and frequent, and unannounced, visits by the district inspector.

The report concluded that the present lighthouse establishment could be sufficiently improved only by placing it in the hands of professional men.[37] Pleasonton wasted no time in writing to his ally at Edgartown, Leavitt Thaxter, asking him to obtain the opinions of as many harbor pilots and captains as possible about the quality of the lights: "I have reason to believe that our Lights are perfectly satisfactory to all navigating people and, if so, their opinions will have more weight than those of persons having no interest in them other than a desire to obtain control of the funds appropriated for Light House purposes." Pleasonton sent the statements gathered by Thaxter to the president, with the comment, "The great object of this attack was to introduce the French lenses into our Light Houses, which do not suit this country and for that reason I opposed and still oppose the employment of them." But his effort failed, and, when the new board was established, Pleasonton lost the position he had held for thirty-two years. The *Vineyard Gazette* commented, "We are very glad to learn that Mr. Pleasonton has lost his office. It is astonishing that our government has kept a regular antediluvian old Granny like Pleasonton in office for almost half a century."[38]

Even then, Congress might not have acted on the legislation proposed by the board except for an incident involving some members of Congress. George Blunt later related the circumstance:

> In 1852, the bill for creating the Light-house Board was pending in Congress, but being opposed by parties interested in keeping up our bad system, its passage was doubtful. The Baltic steamer was then at Washington, and sailed for New York. Off Sandy Hook, she was detained by a fog, and could not run for want of proper buoys. A meeting of the passengers, among who were several members of Congress, was called on board, and their attention particularly directed to this defect, and, on their returning to Washington they

caused the above-named bill to be passed. Punch says, to make railroad travelling safe, put a director on the locomotive. To get a bill through Congress, let the members see the necessity practically.[39]

On 31 August 1852, Congress passed legislation creating a permanent Light House Board. Three members were added to the six of the provisional board, including the secretary of the Treasury as ex officio president and Joseph Henry, first secretary of the Smithsonian and one of the country's leading physicists. All were to serve without remuneration, as did members of the French and Scottish boards.

Establishment of this board marked a turning point for U.S. lighthouses. The system, previously trapped in the careless habits of an earlier time, finally received the benefits of modern management. It had grown haphazardly through assertion of local interests and was a national system in name alone. When change finally came, it arrived with a major advantage: the U.S. Light House Service was able to draw from the best in European lighthouse administrations. At long last, the nation's ablest minds were engaged in making the U.S. system the equal of any in the world.

The U.S. Light House Board continued its work until 1910, by which time the system had grown beyond the ability of an unpaid board to manage it well. Replacement of military inspectors with more permanent civilian inspectors also seemed desirable. That year Congress created a new Bureau of Lighthouses within the Commerce Department and appointed as its commissioner George R. Putnam, an engineer for twenty years with the Coast and Geodetic Survey. Putnam shaped the bureau ably during his twenty-five-year tenure. When he took office, there were nearly fifteen hundred lighthouses and a total of more than eleven thousand aids to navigation of all types. When he retired, the number of aids had doubled while employees decreased nearly 20 percent through automation and electrification. Putnam introduced many improvements, including the use of radio beacons for navigation, the electric buoy, and electric fog signals. In 1918, a retirement system for keepers was begun (a provision based on one made for Scottish keepers in the early nineteenth century).[40]

In 1939, the Bureau of Lighthouses was abolished and its responsibilities transferred to the Coast Guard. Personnel could choose to remain civilians or become Coast Guard employees, and about half chose the latter course. This transfer was economic, bringing all coastal activities under one agency. The Coast Guard has continued to modernize the service, with recent technical improvements including LORAN (long-range navigation) and SHORAN (short-range navigation) and replacement of lightships with huge automatic buoys. In 1970, LAMP (Lighthouse Automation and Modernization Program) was instituted by Congress, for the purpose of eliminating all lighthouse keepers by the end of 1989. Two hundred years after establishment of the U.S. lighthouse system, the profession of lighthouse keeper came to an end.

Keepers and Their Families

I used to have to take [my father] down to the shore; he'd
think he had to go back there to light the light up at
night. . . . I tried to make him understand the light wasn't
there any more. He'd stand on the beach and look and
wait. . . . He couldn't understand why he couldn't see it.
He'd have to go out there and light that light up.

—MYRTLE CORBISHLEY, speaking of her father, Charles Whitford,
keeper of Sabin Point Lighthouse for twenty-four years

Such is the dedication commonly associated with the profession of lighthouse keeping. Virtues such as patience and reliability were indeed the norm for keepers employed by the Light House Service in the late nineteenth and early twentieth centuries. The profession had become respectable, good performance was rewarded with promotion, and appointments were free of political influence. Keepers and their families might remain at a station for many years, becoming part of their community.

Such had not always been the case, as we have seen. Despite the prestige of the position during the colonial period, by the early nineteenth century the status of keepers declined along with the usefulness of the lights. In the absence of a specific body to oversee lighthouse administration, the appointment of keepers became politicized; by mid-century, the spoils system was in full swing, and the alternation of Whig and Democratic party power in presidential politics was felt throughout the civil service. In 1845, when Democrat James Polk became president, Democrat Joseph Pease replaced Whig Leavitt Thaxter as collector of customs on Martha's Vineyard, and Pease appointed Samuel Flanders as keeper at Gay Head. Four years later, the Whigs returned to office with Zachary Taylor, Thaxter replaced Pease, and Henry Robinson replaced Flanders. In 1852, Franklin Pierce returned the Democrats to office, Joseph Pease was reinstated as collector, and Flanders returned to Gay Head. In gratitude, Flanders named his newborn son Franklin Pierce Flanders.[1]

Often those appointed as keepers were the physically disabled or semiskilled, those unfit for other employment. (When women were appointed, it was generally to succeed their disabled or deceased husbands.) In 1850, the customs collector for Newport described some Rhode Island keepers as follows: "The Newport light is kept by a widow, her chief assistant is her son, a slight built lad of 16, and the lighthouse is towards 100' high. Poplar Point is lower but is kept by an elderly man of unwieldy proportions. At Point Judith the keeper is active and in the prime of life, but has the use of but one hand."[2] The lack of other means of employment for such people explains in part the ferocity with which these positions were sometimes contested. A collection of letters (now at the Coast Guard Academy Library in New London, Connecticut) written soon after Polk's election shows how brutal the competition could be. William P. Babcock, keeper of Rhode Island's Dutch Island Lighthouse, fearing that he would be ousted, wrote the secretary of the Treasury:

> Sir, I am informed that there is one or two applicants trying for this light
> house. And I have a desire to inform your honor that I like my situation, and
> should be very sorry to lose it, for I am poor, and it is all I shall have to
> depend on to support my family through the winter. I consider myself noth-
> ing but a servant entirely at your honor's disposal and pleasure. It is hardly 8
> months ago, since I was appointed here to fill a vacancy by a recommendation
> from both parties at the time. If keeping a good light and attending to my
> duty will ensure your honour's approbation, I should be grateful for the
> favor.[3]

One who contested his position was Cyrus Champlin of South Kingstown. Champlin wrote Polk that he was an applicant for the position of keeper of the lighthouse at Point Judith but that, as he understood others wanted the post, he would also accept a position at Dutch Island. He feared, however, opposition to his appointment because he was a "temperance man" and because he voted for General Harrison in 1840, "considering him one of the old republicans who had defended the country and that people ought not forget him in consaquince." Should he be appointed to Dutch Island, he concluded,

> it would be my wishes for to have it come soon it being the season of the
> year that the appointment is of some consaquince, in the winter this appoint-

ment is worth but little it being on a small island and know other hous on it
and the wood being high at that season of the year and sometime rather difficult to get under thos circumstances in case you should see fit to make a
removal.[4]

Christopher A. Sweet hoped to oust keeper Robert Weeden, appointed to Beavertail
a year before Polk's election. He wrote the secretary of the Treasury,

> I understood your honor to say that the appointment was mine, if Weeden's
> politics were in opposition to the administration. This has been proved, and I
> would respectfully call your attention to what you said to me at our inter-
> view. When I returned home, there was a number of men here was ready to
> send on purports to this effect and men of his own party that at times there
> was no light at times in the night, in that light house. I sent very ready by as I
> thought sufficient evidence respecting these facts, and I am apt to think you
> have never received the last documents that I sent, as I have had no answer.[5]

Sweet was unsuccessful. On Weeden's death in 1848, he was succeeded by his
widow, Demaris Weeden, who remained at the lighthouse until 1856.

A final letter, unusual in that its author was a woman, concerns the Point Judith
light. It was written by A. F. Potter in April 1845:

> To the President—Feeling, that I am taking a great liberty, and something
> rather unusual for a female thus to address you. Still I hope you may excuse
> this boldness and take some interest in the subject.
>
> Having been brought up in affluence, and now feeling the want of a good
> living, my friends most of them strong political characters and some of them
> Congressmen, induces me to this bold act.
>
> My husband, Niles Potter, from one of the first families in this place, ap-
> plied for the Office [of keeping] the Point Judith Light. Every way qualified
> keeping as good light as the present man. And although I say it, much more
> popular character, and from much better family.
>
> I hope you will search into the subject as speedily as possible and grant my
> request. My husband on your side altogether. Mr. Hadwin on the other side.
>
> P.S. I beg the favor of your not exposing my thus addressing you as my
> husband would be displeased at this bold act. But thinking a woman's influ-
> ence might avail something.
>
> If you please you may grant this request soon, and you will oblige, your
> most humble servant, A. F. Potter.[6]

Once a keeper's position was secured, though, working conditions could be appalling; not until I. W. P. Lewis's investigation of New England lighthouses in 1842 did anyone at the federal level pay attention to keepers' living conditions. The testimony that keepers gave Lewis makes interesting reading. Ambrose Martin, who tended the Baker's Island twin lights for seventeen years, reported that both towers were so badly cracked that rainwater ran down inside and iced the walls and stairs in the winter. With no ventilation in the lantern, he found it difficult to keep the reflectors clean. Most of the silver had worn off the reflectors anyway, and the chimney holders were so roughly made that glass chimneys broke regularly. His house had rotten sills, leaked badly, and was exceedingly cold in the winter. He kept his cow and hay in the remains of the old beacon, which also leaked so badly that most of the hay had rotted. He lost his boat in a gale the previous year, and it had not been replaced. And, because the government would not fence his land, livestock belonging to other landowners damaged his property and killed his cow.[7]

Many keepers performed their duties as best they could, despite the obstacles. Others did not, and mariners complained often about lights that were tended irregularly or that were extinguished in the course of the night. Supervision was so lax, however, that keepers seldom lost their jobs for dereliction of duty.

Politics was not entirely removed from the system until 1896, when the position of lighthouse keeper became part of the classified civil service, yet the 1852 *Report . . . of the Light House Board* was a clear turning point for the work of keepers as well as for all other aspects of the system. Finally, an organizational structure was created with expectations, rewards, and penalties. The new Light House Service tightened requirements for keepers, provided training, and instituted inspections with penalties for poor performance. For the most serious infraction, allowing the light to be extinguished at night, keepers were now dismissed without recourse. Nominations still were made by the customs collectors but were endorsed by the Light House Board before being forwarded to the secretary of the Treasury. Candidates had to be between eighteen and fifty, be able to read, write, and keep accounts and do the requisite manual labor, pull and sail a boat, and have enough mechanical ability to make minor repairs. After an apprenticeship of three months, candidates were examined by an inspector, who forwarded the results to the Light House Board. Thereupon, candidates were either fully certified or dropped from the service.[8]

Living conditions after 1852 improved steadily. Some stations continued to have only one keeper, but a major light might have one head keeper and up to four assistants, including one who tended the fog signal. The Light House Service showed

Fig. 29. Ida Lewis at Lime Rock Lighthouse, running to perform a rescue. *Harper's Weekly*, 31 July 1869.

concern not only for keepers' physical needs but also for their intellectual needs by circulating portable libraries. By 1889, 550 such libraries were distributed to 1,150 keepers, each containing approximately fifty volumes of what the service considered a "proper admixture of historical, scientific, poetical, and good novels, together with a Bible and a prayerbook." Keepers were prohibited from outside work interfering with lighthouse duties, but many did undertake permitted occupations such as shoemaking, tailoring, or even teaching. Some served as preachers and justices of the peace.[9]

In 1883, uniforms were mandated for all keepers, a fatigue outfit for everyday wear and dress for special occasions that consisted of coat, vest, trousers, and cap (or a helmet for hot climates). The service presented each male keeper then in office with one custom-made suit of each, but subsequently all uniforms were at the owner's expense. No uniform was prescribed for female keepers.[10]

The lives of some keepers are known to us through family folklore, local history, and in some cases legend. One keeper, Ida Lewis, who tended Newport's Lime Rock Lighthouse for more than fifty years, ascended to the level of national heroine.

Fig. 30. Ida Lewis rowing her boat off Lime Rock. Courtesy Newport Historical Society.

In 1854, when Ida was sixteen, her father, Captain Hosea Lewis, was appointed keeper of the new harbor light built on a rocky outcropping a short distance off shore. Three years later, Captain Lewis suffered a stroke, Mrs. Lewis took over as keeper, and Ida took on more of the household work. She rowed the younger children to school and often crossed the harbor on other errands; her oarsmanship thus acquired was the basis of her later fame.

The proximity of Lime Rock to the bustling port and adjacent Fort Adams provided Ida with opportunity for helping many in distress. She performed rescues from time to time with little fanfare. But in 1869 an article in *Harper's Weekly* brought her feats to national attention. It described several occasions of Ida's bravery: the saving of four lads capsized in a small boat; three foolish soldiers who had gone sailing off Fort Adams on a stormy night rescued by Ida; and workmen from a nearby estate whose boat was swamped while they were searching for a sheep (Ida saved the sheep, too). *Harper's* called her "Newport's Grace Darling" after an English lightkeeper's daughter memorialized by Wordsworth, and the idea stuck. Ida's fame grew over the years as she rescued others from the waters of Newport Harbor.

Ida eventually succeeded her mother as keeper and lived out her life at the light. Over the years she received many honors. President Grant, General Sherman, and Susan B. Anthony paid her homage at Lime Rock. Ida continued to tend the light until a few days before her death in 1911, an event mourned by all Newport. Her gravestone with its crossed oars overlooks the harbor from the Falwell Street Cemetery, and her rowboat is displayed at the Newport Historical Society. The lighthouse, decommissioned after her death, today is the Ida Lewis Yacht Club.

Why did this frail-looking woman, who kept her nightly vigil in the midst of Newport's splendor, so capture the imagination of America? The country, prospering after the Civil War, was swelled with a sense of its own grandeur—all the more reason, perhaps, why it eagerly honored this unassuming symbol of its underlying humanity. Once, when asked how she kept her watch every night, Ida replied, "The light is my child, and I know when it needs me, even if I sleep."[11] No other lighthouse is so closely associated with the character of a single person.

As the reforms of the Light House Board took hold, more aspired to a life of lighthouse keeping. Onshore stations were considered good places to live, particularly for families with children. Salaries were modest, but food, especially fish, was plentiful. Sometimes sons succeeded their fathers in the position, and a family might retain stewardship of a lighthouse for two or even three generations. On Block Island, Henry Clark and his son Willett served a total of fifty-five years as first and second keepers of the Southeast light. The Whaley family had a tenure of forty-eight years at Point Judith, beginning with Joseph in 1862 and ending with Henry in 1910. (The family ties grew when Henry Clark married Joseph Whaley's sister. Later, Henry's daughter Bessie married Simeon Dodge, who served as a keeper alongside Willett. Another daughter married Captain Amos Teppo, who served for a time at Point Judith.)

The keepers' wives worked alongside the men. They shared in polishing the brass and cooked for their families and any visiting workmen and on occasion for survivors of shipwrecks. They also scrubbed and kept the quarters clean at all times for "surprise inspections."

The men were responsible for keeping the equipment in order, the lens clean and the wick trimmed, the kerosene font filled, the grounds maintained, and the fences and trim painted. They stood alternate twelve-hour watches and ran up the weather pennants on a pole in case of any change in the forecast.

The keeper maintained the fog horns as well as the light. Because the steam engine that powered the horn took some time to start up, it was important to be

Fig. 31. Keepers and their families at the Southeast light, Block Island, Willett Clark at far left. On the steps is Anna Clark, whose daughter, Jean Caswell Napier, contributed this photograph.

ready when the fog rolled in. Like many keepers, Willett had a sixth sense for knowing when the fog was coming:

> Grandfather would go out several times a day and just stand and listen to the sounds of the water and sort of look at the wind and watch the birds and

Fig. 32. Repair of foghorn, Southeast light. Courtesy of Jean Napier.

different things and then he'd come in and he'd get the fellows that were stationed here and say, "Come on, we've got to go power up the fog horn, the fog is coming." And no one would believe him. And within a couple of hours the fog would come drifting in.

Martin Thompson was keeper of Sandy Point Lighthouse on Prudence Island from 1905 to 1934. His grandson, Charles Homan, lived with Martin and his wife at the light while a small boy. His grandfather's experience was typical of many keepers. Martin was a Scandinavian and, after being wrecked three times in the Norwegian merchant marine, joined the crew of an American vessel. Wrecked again during a hurricane on the Delaware Capes, he decided that he had had enough and got a job

Fig. 33. Martin Thompson, keeper of Sandy Point Lighthouse on Prudence Island, 1905–32.

with the Light House Service in New York. Thompson became assistant keeper first at Rhode Island's Sakonnet Point and then at Borden Flats in Fall River. Finally he was named keeper at Prudence Island. Charles remembers, "We used to visit all the keepers. They were mostly Scandinavians, or Danes, a couple of Greeks, very nice people. In summertime we would have a lot of the keepers down here, . . . and we would go to their places, and there would be clambakes, good times had by all. Ninety-five percent had families, very few single men."

Like many lighthouse children, Charles had a special job—polishing the brass: "In summer we had more visitors, and it was the duty of keepers at the request of visitors to show them the light. The lens was a very beautiful French crystal lens, and it was quite something to see, highly polished, well taken care of, and the brass, too. I can remember my grandfather saying, 'we will polish the brass,' and the 'we' was me!" As Charles got older, he did more general maintenance: painting, cutting grass, whitewashing the fence, and winding the bell at night:

> A typical day would be like this. First, you were up before five o'clock. When day light came you extinguished the light, trimmed the wick, got everything

Fig. 34. Charles Whitford, keeper of Sabin Point Lighthouse, with his friend Adolph Aaronson, keeper of Pomham Rock Lighthouse. Courtesy of Myrtle Corbishley.

ready for next night, took care of the tower, polished the lens, put the cover on, then you went about your duties of painting, maintaining, and general chores; just like on a farm, your work was never done. Then we'd do what we had on the side, pull a lobster pot, some trawling. Toward evening you'd just reverse what you did in the morning. And if you had fog coming, my grandfather would figure, and this I never could understand, but he could feel if the fog was going to set in maybe 2:00 or 3:00 o'clock in the morning, and in that case he'd retire very early, and he would set an alarm to make sure he wouldn't miss, but nine times out of 10 he would be up before the alarm went off. Then the bell would start, the sound was very nice, much better than the hooter we have now.

In those days, the lighthouse was a focal point of the island, a place where people, mariners and others, would gather during any storm or emergency. Sadly, it was

Fig. 35. Sabin Point Lighthouse. Courtesy of Myrtle Corbishley.

this that brought Martin Thompson, by then retired, to the keeper's house during the 1938 hurricane. The tidal wave that swept up the bay struck the keeper's house, and Thompson and four others were drowned.

When Charles Whitford retired as the keeper at Sabin Point Lighthouse in 1946, he had been in the Light House Service for a total of thirty-four years. Though Sabin Point was an offshore light that might have seemed isolated to some, his youngest daughter, Myrtle Corbishley, recalls, "We were never lonely; we were a family light." The Whitfords were known to all the ship's captains, who tooted a greeting as they passed by:

> My father was awfully good to us. . . . It isn't like your father getting up and going to work and leaving you, that was his job, so he was there and when

he took us to shore we'd do what we had to do, like go to school, and he was always there to pick us up at night, so we were very close to my dad, very close. He played games with us and things like that.

One day Myrtle was playing tag with her two sisters:

> I fell overboard once when I was four. . . . Instead of being tagged I jumped overboard. They said I came up dog paddling and that's how I learned to swim. I went right off the dock, we had a big dock. My father came over to get me but he saw me swimmin' so he watched me for awhile. My mother was havin' a fit. But that was me. I was a daredevil. Do somethin' for excitement.

Whitford rowed Myrtle and her sisters to school in East Providence. Later, suitors rowed out to the light, and one, son of the keeper at Warwick, eventually married Myrtle's sister Lillian. Sabin Point Lighthouse was dismantled when the channel to Providence was widened in 1968, and some of its granite blocks were used to build the breakwater of the Edgewood Yacht Club across the Bay.

Frank Jo Raymond (a name adapted from the Lithuanian) was only sixteen when he became a lighthouse keeper. He lived in the Black Rock area of Bridgeport, Connecticut, and since he had already been working for two years, did not have any reservations about misstating his age as the legal minimum of eighteen in his application to join the service. When a few months later he got word of an opening at Latimer Reef Lighthouse, he wasted no time. He rose at three the next morning, caught a train to Stonington, and found a lobsterman to take him in his powerboat to the light, two miles distant. "If I'd had any sense I'd have known to go to the Post Office to find out what to do. A boat was waiting for me!" he laughs. The year was 1923, and Frank stayed at the light eleven years. "It was one of the best things that could have happened to me."

Some young men would have found life at a "sparkplug" light (so named from its appearance) two miles from shore confining, but for Frank it opened up the world. In later life, he became a painter and photographer, documenting life along the Connecticut and Rhode Island coast, and here he got his start in both. He began painting in an unusual way:

Fig. 36. Portrait of Frank Jo Raymond painted by Stephen Macomber. Courtesy of Frank Jo Raymond.

Dick Fricke [another keeper at Latimer Reef] is the one who introduced me to painting. I'd never seen a painting before in my life. He asked me if I had some canvas around. I said sure, I went down to the cellar, found some canvas, and he tacked it to a frame of some kind. He undertook to paint with just the house paints we had there, green, black, bright green, red, dark red, and all that, and he made a nice painting of a square rigged ship. I was amazed, I'd never seen it done, it never occurred to me that, you know, what you saw in magazine illustrations were the result of a painter's work. As a kid in the

Fig. 37. Latimer Reef Lighthouse photographed by Frank Jo Raymond. Courtesy of Frank Jo Raymond.

Black Rock area I had never heard of such a thing as an artist. Fricke was a hell of an artist. He was a good letterer, because his family had a sign-painting business, so that he became like a decorator, he painted nice boats. I went out, found canvases, and paints, and went all over, people gave me paints, and brushes, and things like that. And I started painting. While Dick concentrated on ships and lighthouse illustrations, I tried out different kinds of painting and drawing. He said, "You ever see a museum?" I said, "What's a museum?" So I started a trek every month, I went to Providence, New York, Boston.

Fricke's efforts at the lighthouse did not impress the inspector, however:

Dick actually painted ships right on the walls in the lighthouse. It was beautiful, you know, and would you believe, the inspector told him, "Can't do that." Had to wipe 'em. Who the heck is going to see it, only us, and what would be wrong with a picture, you know? He was a little wise tough guy, who probably didn't know anything about painting.

Frank saved $500 with the idea of quitting the light and attending the Rhode Island School of Design, in Providence. ("Do you know what it cost then? $250!") But he learned to his sorrow that he was not qualified: "I didn't know anything about applying, or high school equivalency, and all that." He managed to take drawing classes, however, and during the Depression was appointed to the Works Progress Administration's art project.

Frank learned about music at the lighthouse as well. A wealthy New London woman, Mrs. Edward S. Harkness, made a gift of about two hundred battery-operated radios to the Light House Service. "We could listen to all this music! Years later, I met her at a party where I was taking pictures, and I thanked her. She was surprised—I don't think anyone had ever thanked her in person." Frank bought a saxophone, taught himself to play, and rowed to the mainland to play jazz at local dance clubs. "Every Friday and Saturday, I don't know for how long."

Frank managed to stay in good physical shape. He would join friends in the Life Saving Service as they kept their watches along the Westerly shore. "I would walk with them, keep them awake. If they didn't punch in they'd lose a day's vacation." He and Fricke worked out an exercise routine at the lighthouse, lifting weights one day and jumping rope the next. "I wouldn't just sit around and smoke like some of them," he comments. And of course the two-mile row to the mainland helped. "I could do it in twenty-five to thirty-five minutes, depending on the weather. Twice I rowed to Montauk and back, thirty miles in one day. And once I rowed to Block Island, six and three-quarter hours. They wouldn't let me row back, but I still want to do that some day!"

As the wife of a lighthouse keeper, Marie Carr was called on to perform tasks unthinkable today. The first post that her husband, Earl, held was on Little Gull Island in Long Island Sound. They lived there with their two small children from 1923 to 1927. To get the groceries—or anything else—Marie had first to row one and a half miles to the Fort Meike Army post on Big Gull and from there be taken by motor launch to New London. Little Gull, Marie reported, was "a good place to go. We were never hungry. Lots of fish and lobster pots!" In 1927, the Carrs moved to the Block Island Southeast light, a step that enabled the children to attend

Fig. 38. Marie Carr at the Southeast light, Block Island, ca. 1942. Courtesy of Marie Carr.

school. Though at first Earl "went down a peg" as assistant to head keeper Willett Clark, when Mr. Clark retired a few years later Earl was promoted. The Carrs lived here until 1943.

Out on Long Island Sound, Marie sometimes found herself in situations that daunted even the soldiers from Fort Meike. One winter day she had gone to the city with the assistant keeper, his wife, and their little boy in order to buy a birthday present for her son. She left Earl and the children alone on the island. A storm blew up on their return, and Marie and the others had to spend the night at Big Gull:

> All night long I sat in the window upstairs watching the lighthouse, so afraid my husband would fall asleep. So I called him about two o'clock in the morning, poor fellow, when I think of it, he was upstairs in the tower, he heard the telephone and had to come down, and I said, "Oh, I thought maybe you fell asleep," he says, "No, I'm still awake." I said "Well, I'm watchin' the lighthouse from here."

Marie was also worried about the assistant keeper's rowboat, which he'd left on the beach:

> So I said to him, "Why don't you go down and pull your boat up?" I had
> been there a long time, and knew about the weather. "Oh," he says, "it's all
> right." So I said to him, "Get a couple of soldiers, they'll help you." No,
> they don't take orders from a keeper's wife, he was one that wouldn't. So the
> next morning we go down, there was no boat, it was smashed up on the
> rocks.

They phoned for the Coast Guard to come from New London and deliver them to the lighthouse, but the assistant keeper's wife, who'd never liked Little Gull anyway, was afraid of the current and wanted to go back to New London. All four got in the motor launch, and the captain went as close to Little Gull as he dared and then asked, "Who's going ashore?" There was a rowboat behind the launch for them to use:

> Well I looked at the assistant keeper thinking he might help Dad, if it was fog
> you know. So, ah, he says, "not me." His wife says, "I don't want to go
> back on that lighthouse!" So I said to the captain, "I'll go, because I've got
> two good children and my husband's on that lighthouse!" Oh, okay. Oh, it
> was a cold day! So here I am pulling (he was a Coast Guard man, he couldn't
> pull a boat, I could do a better job than he could!) and Dad kept on a sayin',
> "Come in, come in, come in!" But we had to turn back. They had to cut the
> gloves off of my hands they were so frozen. My hands were stiff so they took
> snow and rubbed my hands, that's what they do when you freeze your hands.
>
> So the next thing I know, Dad is in the boat, he's comin' out to the Coast
> Guard boat and he has Ruth and Richard, sittin' in the bow of the boat, he
> figured that if anything happened his two children wouldn't be there alone. So
> I went ashore, and the other fellow that was supposed to go ashore went to
> New London on the Coast Guard boat. And it was two days before he could
> get back, before it calmed down enough for him to get back to the
> lighthouse.

Another time a man was bringing her back in the rowboat:

> He got caught in the tide. He went sailing right by that lighthouse! We
> fetched up down on the can buoy, so I thought he was going to have a heart

attack, because he was an older man. Now here I was holdin' on you know, every once and awhile I'd push myself off so the boat wouldn't hit the can buoy. So Dad put Ruth and Richard in the boat and came out between Race Rock Lighthouse and our island to get me again. The sergeant's wife, Mrs. Reddy, she called up she says, "Mrs. Carr, you're never going to die drowning!" Nine lives. I think I did.

The inspectors would show up when least expected:

> I remember one time, it was very early in the morning, it was still a little dark out. Ruth got into bed with me, my husband was on duty, and there was a lightning storm. I was scared stiff, but every time the lightning would flash Ruth would say, "Oh, that's a pretty light! Look at the pretty lightning!" And all of a sudden she says, "Oh, look at the pretty boat!" And there was the lighthouse tender, waiting for 7:30, to come in to the lighthouse to inspect. You *never* knew when they were comin'. They'd inspect everything in the house. The house belongs to *them*. They used to run their fingers along the window sills to see if there was dust. We had one inspector, oh I used to hate him. He'd have a handkerchief and he'd run it over the window by your stove, of all places.
>
> One day I wanted to go to town, and we had to get that boat over on the island there. So what did I do but take my dishes, put my dishes in the dish pan and cover them and put them under the cupboard. I said, gee, if I ever get to the city I'll leave my dishes in the sink! Because I didn't have time to wash them before the boat came. But we didn't have inspection that day.

On 21 September 1938, the great hurricane smashed into the coast:

> My windows were broken in the livingroom. The tower windows were breaking. Everything was going. Somebody says, "Look at the garage!" The garage is gone, the shack is gone. It was scary! The stones came up that bank, up the cliffs there, right into my livingroom, and they went up and hit the tower and put the lights out. So the men went up the tower, they put the dishpans over their heads, and they went up the tower and they had to turn the light by hand, all night long; to get that going, the revolving light.

(The light itself still ran on an emergency generator.) But the hurricane brought some good to the keepers' families:

Fig. 39. Charles Vanderhoop, keeper of Gay Head Lighthouse, Martha's Vineyard, 1920–33. Courtesy of Eloise Page.

We got electric light after that, and I got running water. I went from 1923 to 1938, pumping water. All those years is a good many years to pump water. In a bucket. After the hurricane we got the bathroom on Block Island, this beautiful big bathroom, all white tile trimmed in black. And the reason we got that bathroom was because the hurricane blew everything away. It took the aerial towers and bent them right in half; it blew away the paint shed, corrugated metal; it blew away the garage. And it left the outhouse! That was the only thing left standing. So the men went out the next morning, and pushed it over. We got our bathroom after that!

Charles Vandeerhoop, born on Martha's Vineyard in 1882, was head keeper at Gay Head from 1920 until 1933. His daughter, Eloise Page, was born nearby at her grandmother's house and grew up at the light with her brothers and sisters until she was seventeen. She remembers hers as "a lovely childhood, because we had so much freedom. We went swimming by ourselves, climbed all over the cliffs. We frightened the tourists to death, they knew we were going to fall! We would just balance on the edge of a high cliff and nobody ever got hurt. It's just amazing. Our parents seemed to have no fear that one of us would get hurt."

The difficult living conditions that afflicted some keepers and their families did not pertain to the Vanderhoops. The community of Gay Head was their home long before Mr. Vanderhoop was appointed keeper of the light. "We were happy because we were home, all our relatives were around us," recalls Eloise. Both Charles and his wife, Ethel, were members of the Wampanoag Indian tribe that populated that area of Martha's Vineyard. Charles had earlier been in the Coast Guard but enlisted in the Light House Service at the urging of his wife, who hated him being away from home so often. Eloise remembers happily the time he spent with his family.

Charles could supplement his modest salary by harvesting the wild cranberry bogs he owned in the area. After a good harvest, he would take the family on vacation, making sure that the children had the opportunity to visit Boston, Providence, and other cities. As a member of the close-knit Gay Head community, he could always find someone to substitute for him in his absence.

George Nemetz worked from 1947 to 1962 as a civilian maintaining and repairing lighthouses for the Coast Guard along the coast from Plymouth to Watch Hill. He installed electricity in many and sometimes lived several weeks with keeper families. He often heard good stories. The following anecdote about two keepers at Sakonnet Lighthouse is an extreme version of the kind of cabin fever to which men at such isolated sites were subject:

> There were two keepers out there, Cellers and Fuller, two weeks on and one week off, and they didn't speak to each other. They prepared their food separately, locked their doors when sleeping, and wouldn't talk for months at a time. Well, it was one of those times when they had a terrible, terrible rainstorm in January and turned northwest, blew seventy miles per hour and froze so everything was solid. So, Cellers is sitting with his feet next to the stove and he's reading a book and this is all with the Alladin lamps. Fuller goes outside to make an inspection and he found an icicle three or four feet long and came back in with it in his hand and laid it alongside Celler's neck from the back. Naturally, Cellers got startled, y'know, and he jumped up and he sees Fuller standing with that big, big icicle in his hand and he's brandishing it

Fig. 40. Sakonnet light, an offshore light that can only be reached by boat.

like a sword. Well, Cellers went into the drawer and pulled out a butcher knife and they're going at each other. Around and around the center post, just "Mark of Zorro" type of thing. Naturally, it's hotter than the devil in there, this icicle's starting to melt and Cellers is beating on it with the knife. Sure enough, it broke off and Fuller threw it in Cellers' face and ran outside. Immediately, Cellers locked the door, great big bolts in the door, you know, and barricaded the windows. There were big shutters on the inside and Cellers closed those so Fuller couldn't get in. Fuller stayed outside *two days*. He ran the air compresser motors for the fog horns to keep warm laying over the top. Finally about two days later some fishing boat, after the storm, rescued him. They took him off of there and wouldn't put the two of them together again. Both were taken off the light.

John Ganze spent much of his early working life, from 1926 to 1943, in lighthouses along the coast from New Jersey to Massachusetts. After the Coast Guard took over superintendence of lighthouses, many of the older keepers chose to remain with the Lighthouse Service. Ganze, thirty-nine, chose the Coast Guard. He had suffered through the early years of the Depression in one of the worst possible posts, and he was unequivocal in his assessment of the service: "You could drop dead in winter and no one would find you till spring." Though he'd begun his career as an assistant at New Jersey's Highland light, a comfortable post that he remembers as a "beautiful place," in 1930 he was transferred to Rhode Island's Sakonnet Lighthouse, one-quarter mile offshore at Little Compton. "It was like a smokestack, and very cold," Ganze recalled. "There was only the kitchen stove for warmth and in the winter you had to sleep with four or five blankets. The Treasury Department ran the lighthouses then. They'd give you a cord of wood for the winter and when it ran out—that was it." Other conditions were also grim. Butter could be kept cool in the cistern, but without refrigeration other foods spoiled quickly. Nor was there hot water, of course. Rainwater from the roof was funneled through a pipe to the cistern and was used for drinking as well as other purposes. "Birds would get blown up from the south, canaries and cardinals. They'd see the light flashing and fly at it, hit the roof, break their necks, and then get washed down into the cistern. It might be a year or two before you could get down there to clean it."

For all this, Ganze's pay was only $110 a month, but with the Depression on he was glad even for that. Eventually, he was reassigned to Plum Beach Lighthouse. While this, too, was a "sparkplug" structure, he remembers it with some fondness. The light was located well within the bay and sheltered from the ferocious storms of the more exposed coastline. He could row to shore almost every day and soon had a special reason to do so. On Memorial Day, 1937, he married Margaret Benson, and together they set up an apartment in nearby Saunderstown.

Farming was the main occupation in this rural area. Other activity was provided by the several ferries that carried passengers and freight across the bay. In those days, Narragansett Bay froze over nearly every winter from Dutch Island almost to Providence. "People said you could ride a horse and wagon over the ice." The lights from several other beacons kept him company at night: Wickford to the north, Dutch Island to the east, and Whale Rock to the south.

In the midst of this peaceful life, tragedy struck. In September the great hurricane of 1938, the worst storm of the century, smashed into the Rhode Island coast with little warning. Ganze, inside the lighthouse with substitute keeper Edwin Babcock, was witness to one of the storm's most dramatic losses. "We felt a breeze coming," he recalled in something of an understatement.

Fig. 41. John Ganze at Plum Beach Lighthouse, ca. 1938. Courtesy of Alda Kaye.

We saw the Saunderstown ferry, then we couldn't see that or Whale Rock. Soon the waves were twenty feet high. One came through the kitchen window and pushed the stove to the wall. We kept moving from one floor to another until we got to the third deck. The porthole was open and the wind was coming in, then a wave came in too. It had to have been thirty feet high. Houses and timber were going by; but they didn't hit the light because of the rip-rap around the bottom.

Walter Eberle, keeper at Whale Rock one mile to the south, was not so fortunate. As Ganze described it,

At night, after the storm passed, we looked to see if its light was on, and it wasn't. We looked again in the morning and saw that the lighthouse was gone. The eye of the storm had come right up the bay, hit the lighthouse, broke off the canopy, then got inside and broke up the building. Plum Beach was farther away and the waves had started flattening out by the time they reached us. Whale Rock got the first blast.

Fig. 42. Whale Rock Lighthouse, 1882. Mystic Seaport Museum.

In many ways, the 1938 hurricane was a forewarning of the end of an era marked the following year by the Coast Guard's taking charge of the lighthouse system. In Rhode Island, several lighthouses damaged in the storm were discontinued soon after. Although the decline in shipping and use of passenger steamers during the Depression had brought the golden age of lighthouse keeping to an end some time before, changes to come would make the very existence of many lighthouses only a memory. Even before the hurricane, the Plum Beach light had been scheduled to be decommissioned, for the new Jamestown Bridge would serve as a navigational signal without the expense of a keeper. The Mount Hope Bridge further up the Bay had already made the Bristol Ferry light obsolete. The United States' entry into World War II was the biggest change of all. When the war was over, civilian keepers were rapidly replaced by those serving in the Coast Guard. Henceforth, keepers seldom stayed at a light for more than three or four years, and lighthouse keeping alternated with other tours of duty. Families continued to live at many lighthouses and form close attachments to "their" lights. But never again was keeping the light burning a profession and a way of life.

Fig. 43. Whale Rock Lighthouse after 1938 hurricane. Courtesy of Wilfred Warren.

CATALOG OF LIGHTS

Massachusetts Lights

Active

Date immediately following name is when the light was first lit.

Annisquam Harbor Light, 1801
Annisquam. Located on Wigwam Point on the east side of the harbor. The original keeper's house and oil house remain, though the tower was rebuilt in 1897.

Baker's Island Light, 1798
Salem. Built as a twin light to replace a wooden beacon erected by the Salem Marine Society seven years before. Rebuilt in 1815 as a single stone tower, but mariners were confused by the change, and a second tower was added a few years later. Of unequal heights, the two towers were known familiarly as Mr. and Mrs. Baker. Only a single tower remains today.

Bass River Light, 1855
West Dennis. The light was decommissioned in 1914 when the Cape Cod Canal was built. In 1938, Mr. and Mrs. Everett Stone decided to open it as The Lighthouse Inn, still operated today by the same family.

Borden Flats Light, 1881
Fall River. A cast iron conical structure located south of the Braga Bridge.

Boston Light
Courtesy of U.S. Coast Guard

Boston Light, 1716

Boston. The first lighthouse in North America, it was damaged by the British during the Revolution and rebuilt in 1783. In 1859, the tower was raised fourteen feet to its present height, eighty-nine feet above ground level. In 1989, Congress voted that the Boston light would remain permanently manned; it is the only manned lighthouse in the country today.

Brant Point Light
Courtesy of Charles M. Silverman

Brant Point Light, 1746

Nantucket. A small harbor light originally established by the town of New Sherbourne. The light suffered numerous disasters and was rebuilt many times. In 1901, because of the shifting of the harbor channel, the present wooden tower was built on the west side of the harbor entrance.

Butler Flats Light, 1898

New Bedford. This caisson structure replaced the Clark's Point Lighthouse, erected in 1804. Maintained by the city as a private aid to navigation.

Cape Ann (Thacher's Island) Light
Courtesy of U.S. Coast Guard

Cape Ann (Thacher's Island) Light, 1771

Rockport. Established as forty-five-foot twin towers. Rebuilt in 1861 as 124-foot granite towers fitted with first-order Fresnel lenses. The Thacher's Island Association is managing the island in cooperation with the U.S. Coast Guard and U.S. Fish and Wildlife Service. It recently relit the northern light, discontinued in 1932, as a private aid to navigation and is restoring other buildings. The group also operates a launch for visitors. Contact the Thacher's Island Association, P.O. Box 73, Rockport, MA 01966.

Cape Poge Light
Courtesy of U.S. Coast Guard

Cape Poge Light, 1801

Edgartown, Martha's Vineyard. The tower has been moved several times as the coastline eroded. The present structure dates from 1893.

Chatham Light
Courtesy of Charles M. Silverman

Chatham Light, 1808

Chatham. First built as wooden twin lights and rebuilt in the 1830s as brick twin lights. In 1877, the threat of erosion led to the erection of two cast iron towers at a safer location. In 1923, the south tower was moved to North Eastham to replace the last of the Three Sisters at Nauset Beach, and only a single tower remains today. Its Fresnel lens may be seen at the Chatham Historical Society.

Cleveland Ledge Light, 1943

Bourne. Located two miles off shore, it serves vessels near the west end of the Cape Cod Canal. Its modern style suits the last light to be established in Massachusetts. The ledge was named after President Cleveland, who enjoyed fishing in the area.

Cuttyhunk Light, 1823

Cuttyhunk Island, off New Bedford. In 1860, a second story was added to the house, raising the light tower which arose from the roof by ten feet. In 1892 the structure was torn down and a new house and tower were completed the following year. In 1947, both were demolished and a skeleton tower erected.

Deer Island Light, 1890

Winthrop. The present fiberglass tower replaced the original cast iron structure in 1983.

Derby Wharf, 1871

Salem. Located at the end of the nearly half-mile-long Derby Wharf, it was one of three lights established at that time in the vicinity (Fort Pickering and Hospital Point were the others). Lacking keeper's quarters, the twelve-foot-square twenty-five-foot-high tower was tended by a lamplighter. Decommissioned in 1977 and transferred to the National Park Service, it has been restored by Friends of Salem Maritime working with the Peabody Museum of Salem, the U.S. Coast Guard, and the National Park Service. Relit by the Coast Guard in 1983.

Duxbury Pier Light, 1871

Duxbury. In 1984, when the Coast Guard announced plans to replace the top of this conical cast iron tower with a more modern structure, the Bug Light Preservationists raised money and restored the existing lantern.

East Chop Light, 1877.

Oak Bluffs, Martha's Vineyard. A private light was maintained here for many years before this one was established by the government. Today it is surrounded by a city park.

Eastern Point Light
Courtesy of U.S. Coast Guard

Eastern Point Light, 1832

Gloucester. The present tower, the third on the site, was built in 1890.

Edgartown Light, 1828

Martha's Vineyard. The present tower, dating from 1875, was brought here from Ipswich in 1939.

Fort Pickering Light, 1871

Salem. Today part of Winter Island Park and maintained as a private aid to navigation.

Gay Head Light
Courtesy of Charles M. Silverman

Gay Head Light, 1799

Gay Head. Originally built as a wooden octagonal tower. Despite its importance at the entrance to Vineyard Sound, for many years the beacon was barely adequate to the task. When the present brick tower was built in 1856, a first-order Fresnel lens was installed, composed of 1,008 prisms of glass. The lens was replaced in 1953. It is exhibited today at the Duke's County Historical Society. The keeper's house and other buildings have been destroyed.

The Graves
Courtesy of U.S. Coast Guard

The Graves, 1903

Boston. Larger vessels required new channels into Boston Harbor, and this major light was established to guide their way. Its first-order Fresnel lens was removed in 1975 when the light was automated and donated to the Smithsonian Institution.

Great Point Light, 1784

Nantucket. The wooden tower was destroyed by fire in 1816 and rebuilt of stone two years later. In 1984, a storm destroyed the tower, which has been replaced with a replica built with a $1 million congressional appropriation. It has a steel-cellular-cofferdam to protect it from future erosion and is powered by solar panels.[1]

Highland Light, 1798

Truro. Also known as the Cape Cod light and, in earlier times, the Clay Pounds light. Important to vessels crossing the Nantucket Shoals as well as those arriving from Europe. In 1857, threatened by erosion, the tower was rebuilt six hundred feet back from the original site and received a first-order Fresnel lens. Today, only three acres remain of the original ten, and the light is a modern beacon.

Hospital Point Light, 1871

Beverly. Since 1927, it has served as a range light along with a light in the steeple of the First Baptist Church of Beverly.

Ipswich Light, 1838

Ipswich. Originally established as brick twin lights, one of these was replaced with an iron tower in 1875. The front range light was discontinued in 1932 and moved to Edgartown in 1939.

Long Island Head Light, 1820

Boston. The present tower dates from the late nineteenth century.

Long Point Light, 1827
Provincetown. Rebuilt in 1875 and identical with the Wood End Lighthouse one mile away. It is a landmark for visitors to the Cape Cod National Seashore.

Marblehead Light, 1833
Marblehead. The unique cylindrical structure that stands today was built in 1895.

Minot's Ledge Light
Courtesy of Charles M. Silverman

Minot's Ledge Light, 1850
Cohasset. Many a vessel was wrecked on the treacherous Cohasset Rocks before this light was established. It was the first "rock" lighthouse to be built in the United States. Since the reef on which it stands is covered by water at high tide, construction could take place only at low tide and in calm weather. The first tower stood precariously on nine wrought iron stilts and was destroyed in a storm in 1851. The present ninety-seven-foot granite tower was completed in 1860. Since 1894, the light signal has flashed in a 1-4-3 sequence, and local residents have opposed all efforts to change their "I-love-you" (-/- - - -/- - -) signal. The Cohasset Historical Society Museum has exhibits on the lighthouse.

Nauset Beach Light
Courtesy of National Archives

Nauset Beach Light, 1838
North Eastham. Originally established as a triple light with fifteen-foot towers, 150 feet apart. Known as "the three sisters," in 1892 the crumbling stone towers were replaced by three wooden ones thirty feet inland. Two were discontinued in 1911. The present single tower was moved here from Chatham in 1923. In the 1980s, the National Park Service returned the dispersed wooden towers to their original site and restored them as part of the Cape Cod National Seashore.[2]

Ned Point Light, 1837

Mattapoisett. The present tower, built in 1888, is the center of a park operated by the Town of Mattapoisett.

Newburyport Harbor Light, 1873

Newburyport. Established as part of a pair of range lights for guidance of mariners through the channel into Newburyport harbor. Discontinued in 1961, and the front range light moved from Bayley's Wharf to its present location at the Coast Guard station. The rear range light is a private residence.

Newburyport Twin Lights, 1788

Newburyport. Originally established by the Commonwealth of Massachusetts to mark the entrance to the Merrimack River, the small wooden towers could be moved and repositioned when the channel shifted. The present single tower was built in 1898.

Nobska Point Light
Courtesy of Charles M. Silverman

Nobska Point Light, 1828

Falmouth. Replaced in 1876 with a cylindrical iron tower, the light and Coast Guard buildings are familiar landmarks to users of Woods Hole.

Plymouth Light
Courtesy of Charles M. Silverman

Plymouth Light, 1769

Plymouth. Known also as the Gurnet Point Lighthouse, it was the first twin light in the colonies. The wooden towers were destroyed by fire in 1801 and replaced temporarily by a single beacon. They were rebuilt as twin towers the following year and one more time in 1842. One light was discontinued in 1924.[3]

Race Point Light, 1816

Provincetown. Originally constructed of stone, in 1876 it was rebuilt as a cast iron conical tower. Today it is part of the Cape Cod National Seashore.

Sankaty Head Light
Courtesy of Charles M. Silverman

Sankaty Head Light, 1850

Nantucket. Funded by a special act of Congress following discovery of the Davis Southern Shoals, it was the first U.S. light to have a Fresnel lens installed at the time of construction; after reform of the lighthouse administration two years later, use of such lenses became universal throughout the system. In 1950, the lens was moved to the island's Whaling Museum.

Straitsmouth Island Light, 1835

Rockport. The Coast Guard maintains the tower while the Massachusetts Audubon Society manages the island as a bird sanctuary.

Tarpaulin Cove Light
Courtesy of Charles M. Silverman

Tarpaulin Cove Light, 1817

Naushon Island. The present tower was built in 1856. The keeper's house and other buildings have been demolished.

Ten Pound Island Light, 1821

Gloucester. Replaced in 1832 by the Eastern Point Lighthouse and rebuilt at a better location. Relit in 1989 as a private aid to navigation.

West Chop Light, 1817

Vineyard Haven, Martha's Vineyard. The present tower was built in 1891.

Wood End Light
Courtesy of Charles M. Silverman

Wood End Light, 1864
Provincetown. The present tower was built in 1873 and is identical with the nearby Long Point Lighthouse.

Inactive

Billingsgate Island Light, 1822
Wellfleet. In 1915, the sea began to destroy the island and the light. A temporary beacon was erected but discontinued in 1922. Today this island, thirty acres in size when the Pilgrims arrived, has disappeared.

Bird Island Light, 1819
Marion. This light at Sippican harbor near Buzzard's Bay has been restored by the Sippican Historical Society. The island is a nesting ground for roseate terns and piping plovers.

Bishop and Clerks Light, 1858
West Yarmouth, off Point Gammon. When established, the light replaced a lightship. Discontinued in 1928, and demolished in 1952.

Clark's Point Light
Courtesy of National Archives

Clark's Point Light, 1804
New Bedford. Replaced by the Butler Flats caisson light in 1898. The Clark's Point tower has been moved to the top of nearby Fort Taber.

Dumpling Rock Light
Courtesy of National Archives

Dumpling Rock Light, 1828
Dartmouth. Replaced by a navigational marker.

Egg Rock Light, 1856
Swampscott. Destroyed in 1922.

Hyannis Light, 1849
Hyannis. A privately built navigational aid, today it is a private residence.

Lovells Island, 1903
Destroyed in 1939.

Mayos Beach Light, 1838
The light was temporarily discontinued in 1875, and a new tower and house were completed, away from the eroding beach, in 1877. The light was discontinued in 1922. Today the tower is gone and the keeper's house is a private residence.

Monomoy Light
Courtesy of National Archives

Monomoy Light, 1823
Chatham. Located at the southern end of Monomoy Island southeast of Chatham, the light was discontinued in 1923. It is now part of the Monomoy National Wildlife Refuge, and the tower is being restored by the U.S. Fish and Wildlife Service.

The Narrows
Courtesy of National Archives

The Narrows, 1855
Boston. Destroyed by fire in 1929.

Palmer Island Light, 1849
New Bedford. This light, established when the city was at its peak as a whaling port, appears on the city seal. Discontinued in 1941 when replaced by the Butler Flats light.

Pamet Harbor Light, 1849
Truro. Discontinued 1856.[4] Destroyed.

Point Gammon Light, 1816
West Yarmouth. Discontinued in 1858 and now privately owned.

Sandy Neck Light, 1826
Barnstable. The present tower was built in 1857. The lantern room has been removed.

Scituate Light
Courtesy of Charles M. Silverman

Scituate Light, 1811

Scituate. The original lighthouse remains, though altered in 1827, 1847, and 1930. Discontinued in 1860 after Minot's Ledge light was established. Restored in the 1920s, today it is maintained by the Scituate Historical Society.

Spectacle Island Range Lights, 1897

Boston.

Stage Harbor Light, 1880

Chatham. Replaced by a white skeleton tower in 1933. The lantern room has been removed.

Wing's Neck Light, 1849

Bourne. Rebuilt in 1889. Today it is a private residence.

Rhode Island Lights

Active

Beavertail Light
Courtesy of Newport Historical Society

Beavertail Light, 1749

Jamestown. The first lighthouse at Beavertail was the third in the colonies. Made of wood, it burned to the ground four years later. The rubble stone tower that replaced it was damaged by retreating British in 1779. The light was relit in 1783, and the structure remained notoriously drafty until replaced by the present granite tower in 1856. In 1817, Newport inventor David Melville conducted an unusual experiment in lighting the beacon with gas, but expansion of his efforts was thwarted by opposition of the whale oil industry. The assistant keeper's house, added in 1898, today houses the Beavertail Lighthouse Museum (open mid-June–Labor Day, Wednesday–Sunday).

Castle Hill Light
Courtesy of Charles M. Silverman

Castle Hill Light, 1890

Newport. Originally constructed with a keeper's house a short distance away, today it is operated from the nearby Castle Hill Coast Guard Station. Its construction was delayed for many years by opposition of landowner and noted naturalist Alexander Agassiz, who resented the encroachment on his property. Steamboat companies, meanwhile, painted the rocky cliffs white for the safety of vessels at night.

Conimicut Light, 1868

Off Warwick. In 1883, the present conical cast iron tower replaced a wooden predecessor destroyed by ice floes. In 1960, Conimicut was the last lighthouse to be electrified in the United States.

Goat Island Light, 1839

Newport. The light was located at the end of a long pier to mark a reef north of the island, and its predecessor stood unlit for many years (see *Sandy Point Light*). After the Civil War, Goat Island was the home of a naval torpedo factory. In the early 1920s, a torpedo boat made a bad landing and struck the keeper's house, which then was demolished. Today the island has been filled in and is primarily occupied by the Goat Island Sheraton Inn.

Hog Island Shoal Light
Courtesy of Charles M. Silverman

Hog Island Shoal Light, 1901

Off Portsmouth. This lighthouse, the last to be established in Rhode Island, replaced a lightship maintained by the Lighthouse Service since 1886.

North Light
Courtesy of Charles M. Silverman

North Light, 1829

Block Island. Four successive lights have warned vessels away from the treacherous reef extending north of the island. The first, a stone double light, was situated too close to the beach. Threatened by erosion, it was replaced in 1837 by another twin light, this time too far inland to do its job well. In 1856, a single tower was built nearer the water, but this was once again threatened by erosion. The last time the job was done right, with a sturdy stone building resembling that at Norwalk. Paving stones were added to retard the shifting action of the dunes. The light was decommissioned in 1955 and subsequently vandalized. Today it is being restored as a museum by the North Light Commission, which has installed a solar-powered light as a private aid to navigation.[5]

Point Judith Light
Courtesy of U.S. Coast Guard

Point Judith Light, 1810

Narragansett. A beacon marked this site in colonial times. The first lighthouse, of wood, was destroyed in the great gale of 1816. Its stone replacement stood until the present octagonal granite tower was constructed in 1856. The keeper's house was removed in the 1950s.

Sandy Point Light
Courtesy of RI Department of
Environmental Management

Sandy Point Light, 1852

Prudence Island, Portsmouth. This lighthouse was built in 1823 on Goat Island, where it was unlit for many years following its replacement in 1839. It was moved in 1851 and lit the following year. It is the oldest standing lighthouse in Rhode Island and its bird cage lantern the only such example in the state.

Southeast Light
Courtesy of RI Department of
Environmental Management

Southeast Light, 1873

Block Island. This magnificent brick structure, first lit in 1875, was erected as part of a larger effort to improve navigation to and around Block Island. Its first-order Fresnel lens is one of the primary lights of the Northeast. The Mohegan Bluffs on which it stands are fast eroding, and the Southeast Light Foundation hopes to move the building back from danger and to restore it as a museum.

Warwick Light
Courtesy of U.S. Coast Guard

Warwick Light, 1827

Warwick. Marking the narrow passage between the northern end of Patience Island and the west shore of Narragansett Bay, the first lighthouse stood for more than a century. In 1932, threatened by erosion, it was replaced by the present conical tower. Following the 1938 hurricane, the lighthouse was moved to its present site at a higher elevation.

Inactive

Bristol Ferry Light, 1854
Bristol. Before the lighthouse was built by the government, the Fall River Steamboat Company maintained a beacon at the site for the guidance of its vessels on the Fall River run. It was decommissioned in 1929 when made obsolete by the new Mount Hope Bridge; today it is a private residence.

Bullock's Point Light, 1872
East Providence. First established as a beacon, a new lighthouse with dwelling was completed in 1876. It was badly damaged by the 1938 hurricane, discontinued, and replaced by a steel tower.

Conanicut North Light, 1886
Jamestown. The lantern has been removed, and the building is now a private residence.

Dutch Island Light
Courtesy of Charles M. Silverman

Dutch Island Light, 1826
Off Jamestown. The island served as a trading post for the Dutch in the seventeenth century. Today the lighthouse is part of the Bay Islands State Park.

Fuller Rock/Sassafras Point Beacon Lights, 1872
Off Jamestown. These wood framed hexagonal beacons marked the east and west sides of the Providence River channel as it neared the city. The keeper rowed out twice daily, braving current, wind, fog, and passing vessels. In 1912, the channel was widened and Sassafras Point demolished. In 1923, an explosion of an acetylene tank that fueled the by-then automatic beacon destroyed the tower, and it was replaced by a steel skeleton tower.[6]

Gould Island Light, 1889

Off Portsmouth. The light replaced a private light operated by the Old Colony Steamboat Company. Often obscured by trees, the lighthouse was discontinued in 1947 and replaced by a skeleton tower with an acetylene beacon. The lighthouse and keeper's dwelling have been destroyed.[7]

Gull Rocks Light, 1887

Newport. This unusual A-frame structure was made obsolete by construction of the Newport Bridge and destroyed in 1970.

Lime Rock/Ida Lewis Light, 1854

Newport. Famous as the home of the American heroine Ida Lewis. Ida's father was the first keeper, succeeded by Ida's mother and eventually by Ida herself. In the course of her fifty-five years at the light, Ida rescued at least eighteen persons from Newport Harbor. In 1925, fourteen years after her death, the light was renamed in her honor. It was discontinued in 1927, and today is the home of the Ida Lewis Yacht Club.

Musselbed Shoal Light, 1873

Portsmouth. The light was rebuilt in 1879 and again in 1920, following damage from ice floes. After further damage by the 1938 hurricane, it was replaced by a steel skeleton tower.

Nayatt Point Light, 1828

Barrington. The present structure was built in 1856, following damage of the building by a storm. Today the light is a private residence.

Plum Beach Light, 1887

Off North Kingstown. Following many delays, the light was finally established after the steamer *Rhode Island* ran aground nearby in a fog. Decommissioned in 1940 following completion of the Jamestown Bridge, today it is an orphan, disowned by the Coast Guard and unclaimed by any others.

Pomham Rock Light
Courtesy of Charles M. Silverman

Pomham Rock Light, 1871
East Providence. Today the lighthouse is owned by the Mobil Oil Company, which maintains a nearby storage facility.

Poplar Point Light, 1831
Wickford, North Kingstown. It was replaced in 1886 by the Wickford Harbor light; today it is a private residence.

Rose Island Light
Courtesy of Newport This Week,
Edie Rose, photographer

Rose Island Light, 1870
Newport. Before the light was established, a man hired by the steamboat companies rowed out to blow a horn in foggy weather. The light was decommissioned in 1971 following completion of the Newport Bridge, and today it is being restored as a museum by the Rose Island Lighthouse Foundation.

Sabin Point Light, 1871
Off East Providence. This light was dismantled in 1968 to facilitate widening of the channel of the Providence River, and some of its granite blocks were used in the pier of the Edgewood Yacht Club.

Sakonnet Light
Courtesy of Orson St. John

Sakonnet Light, 1884

Little Compton. Though authorized for West Island, the light was constructed on the less suitable Cormorant Rock. Purportedly, the original location was opposed by a fish and gun club occupying the island, whose members included such powerful figures as J. P. Morgan. The light was decommissioned after damage in the 1954 hurricane. The sixty-six-foot cast iron tower has been handsomely restored by the Friends of Sakonnet Light and may be relit as a private navigational aid.

Watch Hill Light, 1808

Westerly. The first lighthouse, a cylindrical wooden tower, stood until 1856, when replaced by a square granite tower resembling that built at Beavertail the same year. The light was decommissioned in 1987, and the Watch Hill Improvement Society is restoring the keeper's house as a museum.

Whale Rock Light, 1882

Off Narragansett. This conical cast iron structure was destroyed in the 1938 hurricane, and no trace was ever found of the lighthouse, the bell, or the keeper, Walter Eberle.

Wickford Harbor Light, 1882

Wickford, North Kingstown. Lighted the same day Poplar Point light was discontinued. Replaced in 1930 by a steel structure with automatic light, the picturesque Victorian structure was destroyed soon after.

Connecticut Lights

Active

Faulkner's Island Light, 1802

Faulkner's Island Light
Courtesy of J. E. Helander

Off Guilford. The second light established in Connecticut. Constructed as an octagonal tower of hammered brownstone by Abisha Woodward, who made his reputation by rebuilding the New London lighthouse the previous year. In 1865, Joseph Henry, secretary of the Smithsonian Institution and chairman of the Lighthouse Board, conducted experiments here on the range and audibility of fog signals. The light was automated in 1976 after fire destroyed the 1871 keeper's house. The island was transferred to the U.S. Fish and Wildlife Service in 1985 and is maintained as a nesting ground for colonies of roseate and common terns.[8]

Greens Ledge Light, 1902

Norwalk. Built at the western end of the Norwalk archipelago at a time when increasing use of Norwalk Harbor required more than the Sheffield light.[9]

Latimer Reef Light, 1884

Off North Stonington. Light vessels had marked the area since 1837.[10]

Lynde Point Light
Courtesy of U.S. Coast Guard

Lynde Point Light, 1802

Old Saybrook. The first tower, of wood, was only thirty-five feet high, and its light was often obscured by mist. It was rebuilt in 1838 as a sixty-five-foot octagonal stone tower. Refurbished in 1868, the handsome spiral wooden stair dates from that time. Its fixed fifth-order lens is one of the two Fresnel lenses still in use in Connecticut.

New London Harbor Light, 1760

New London. This octagonal stone tower, sixty-four feet high, was the fourth in the colonies. In 1801, it was rebuilt as an eighty-foot tower, the one that stands today. Its fourth-order Fresnel lens is one of only two Fresnel lenses in Connecticut (the other is at Lynde Point). In the later mid-nineteenth century, the lighthouse was a site for the testing of fog signal equipment, including the Daboll trumpet invented by a New Londoner.

New London Ledge Light, 1910

New London. This cube-shaped brick structure, with mansard roof topped by a lantern, is well known to users of New London Harbor. Such revival-style architecture is unusual for off-shore lights of this period, which were generally of prefabricated cast iron construction. Today the building is used for maritime programs sponsored by Project Oceanography, and the Coast Guard maintains the automated beacon.[11]

Peck Ledge Light, 1906

Norwalk. Conical cast iron tower, established at the eastern end of the Norwalk Island archipelago when the Sheffield light was judged inadequate for the increasing traffic of Norwalk Habor.[12]

Penfield Reef Light, 1874
Off Fairfield. Established to guide the increasing traffic of Bridgeport Harbor following the Civil War.[13]

Saybrook Breakwater Light, 1886
Old Saybrook. Cast iron conical tower standing at south end of jetty extending southward from Lynde Point. Its establishment was part of a wider effort to improve the navigation of Long Island Sound.[14]

Southwest Ledge Light
Courtesy of National Archives

Southwest Ledge Light, 1877
New Haven. Marks hazardous underwater rocks on east side of the main channel into New Haven Harbor. The prefabricated cast iron tube foundation filled with rocks and cement is one of the earliest remaining examples of this type of construction. This design was developed by Major George H. Elliot of the Lighthouse Board for northern underwater sites subject to danger from ice floes. The cast iron superstructure in Second Empire style represents an unusual transition from the more common type of Victorian lighthouse to simpler cast iron towers. Before the superstructure was attached to the foundation, it was exhibited at the Centennial Exhibition in Philadelphia, accompanied by a keeper who lived inside and tended the lamp nightly.[15]

Stratford Point Light, 1822
Stratford. In 1881, the wooden tower was rebuilt as a thirty-five-foot conical cast iron tower, the first in Connecticut and one of the earliest in the country. The original wood-framed keeper's house still stands, as does the 1881 fog signal building.

Stratford Shoal Light, 1877
Stratford.

Tongue Point Light, 1895
Bridgeport.

Inactive

Avery Point Light, 1944
Groton. The last light to be erected in Connecticut, it was discontinued in 1967.

Bridgeport Harbor Light, 1871
Bridgeport. The wooden tower was replaced by a skeleton tower in 1953 and destroyed.

Chatham Ledge Light, 1881
Stamford. Discontinued in 1953 and vacant for many years. In 1985, the seventy-seven-foot conical cast iron tower was privately purchased.

Fayerweather Island Light, 1808
Bridgeport. Also known as Black Rock light. The first wooden lighthouse was destroyed in a storm and replaced in 1823 by the present stone octagonal tower. Discontinued in 1933 and neglected for many years, it has been restored by Friends of Seaside Park.

Five Mile Point Light, 1805
New Haven. The original thirty-foot octagonal tower was rebuilt as a sixty-five-foot stone octagonal tower in 1847. Discontinued when the Southwest Ledge Lighthouse was established in 1877, today it is the focus of the city's Lighthouse Point Park.

Great Captain Island Light, 1829
Greenwich. In 1868, a stone structure resembling the Norwalk and Block Island North lighthouses replaced the original tower and keeper's house. It was decommissioned in 1970 and is now maintained as part of a city park.

Morgan Point Light, 1831
Noank. Rebuilt in 1868 as a two-story granite structure with the tower emerging from the front of the house. Discontinued in 1919.

New Haven Harbor Light, 1804
New Haven. Discontinued in 1877 when superceded by the Southwest Ledge light.

Sheffield Island Light
Courtesy of Norwalk Seaport Association

Sheffield Island Light, 1826
Norwalk. Replaced by a masonry tower in 1868. Discontinued in 1902 when replaced by the Greens Ledge Lighthouse. The Norwalk Seaport Association has restored the lighthouse and operates it as a museum. The island is also a bird sanctuary. For ferry schedule and other information, contact the Norwalk Seaport Association, 92 Washington St., South Norwalk, CT 06854; 203-838-9444.

Stonington Harbor Light, 1824
Stonington. Originally, the light was located further out on the point, but erosion led to its relocation in 1840. This thirty-five-foot tower with attached keeper's dwelling was built by I. W. P. Lewis using stones from the original light. It was decommissioned in 1889 with erection of a breakwater light further out in the harbor. The Stonington Historical Society Museum occupies the building and exhibits the sixth-order Fresnel lens that lit the light for more than thirty years. The museum is open May–October, Tuesday–Sunday, and by appointment.

NOTES AND BIBLIOGRAPHY

Notes

Chapter 1: Bonfires, Beacons, and Colonial Lighthouses

1. Douglas B. Hague and Rosemary Christie, *Lighthouses: Their Architecture, History and Archeology* (Llandysul Dyfed, Wales: Gomer Press, 1975), 33. Seven miles was the maximum distance from which a large bonfire was likely to be seen. John Naish, *Seamarks; Their History and Development* (London: Stanford Maritime, 1985), 85–86.

2. Wayne Wheeler, "The Eddystone, Pt. 1," *Keeper's Log* 1, no. 4 (Summer 1985): 14.

3. More specifically, a parabola is a curve possessing the property that a line drawn from the focus of the light to any point in the curve makes with a tangent at that point an angle equal to that which a line parallel to the axis of the curve makes with that tangent. Alan Stevenson, *A Rudimentary Treatise on the History, Construction, and Illumination of Lighthouses* (London: John Weale, 1850), 79–80.

4. D. Alan Stevenson, *The World's Lighthouses before 1820* (London: Oxford University Press, 1959), 66, 68; Hague and Christie, *Lighthouses*, 164.

5. Naish, *Seamarks*, 25ff.

6. Hague and Christie, *Lighthouses*, 28.

7. Frances Manwaring Caulkins, *History of New London, Connecticut, from the first Survey of the Coast in 1612, to 1850* (New London, Conn., 1852), 381.

8. Arthur H. Gardner, comp., *A List of the Wrecks around Nantucket"* (Nantucket, Mass., 1877), 5.

9. Amelia Forbes Emerson, *Early History of Naushon Island* (1935; 2d ed., Boston: Howland & Co., 1981), 303. This same Lumbert may be the subject of a story recounted by Gail Nemetz in "Lore Connected with Lighthouses along the New England Coastline" (1974, typescript): "At Tarpaulin cove there was a keeper by the name of Lumbert. . . . He was a little money hungry, and ready for an easy dollar. There was a schooner manned by unscrupulous men, who could well be called pirates. They would bribe Lumbert to turn off the light on certain dark nights when they knew a good prize would be bound out of the sound. The unsuspecting ship would keep on coming and run ashore on the rocks, whereupon the people would take to the lifeboats and go ashore. The pirates then would, by the law of salvage, plunder the vessel."

10. William Allen, *Accounts of Shipwreck and of Other Disasters at Sea, Designed To Be Interesting and Useful to Mariners, with an Appendix, Containing Dr. Payson's Address to Seamen,*

and a Few Prayers for Their Use (Brunswick, Maine: Printed by Joseph Griffin, 1823), iv.

11. "Letter from Dr. Benjamin Franklin to Mr. Alphonsus le Roy . . . Containing Sundry Maritime Observations," in *The Writings of Benjamin Franklin,* vol. 9, ed. Albert Henry Smyth (New York: Macmillan Co., 1906), 372. It would seem that this advice on shipbuilding was not heeded, for "A Friend of Seamen" commented in 1823, "In a few years the present method of sending ships to sea with only a single plank to separate between life and death will be ranked among exploded and astonishing absurdities." Allen, *Accounts of Shipwreck.*

12. "Letter from Dr. Benjamin Franklin to Mr. Alphonsus le Roy," 394–96.

13. Alexander Starbuck, *History of the American Whale Fishery from Its Earliest Inception to the Year 1876* (New York: Argosy-Antiquarian, 1964), 55–56.

14. Samuel Eliot Morison, *The Maritime History of Massachusetts, 1783–1860* (Boston: Houghton Mifflin, 1961), 37–38.

15. Philip C. F. Smith, "The Salem Marine Society, 1766–1966," *American Neptune* 26 (1966): 273.

16. Walter Muir Whitehill, *The East India Marine Society and the Peabody Museum of Salem: A Sesquicentennial History* (Salem, Mass.: Peabody Museum, 1949), 179–80.

17. William A. Baker, *A History of the Boston Marine Society, 1742–1967* (Boston: Boston Marine Society, 1968), 68.

18. Ibid., 84–86.

19. Smith, "The Salem Marine Society," 275.

20. Edmund March Blunt, *The American Coast Pilot* (Newburyport, Mass., 1796), title page.

21. Salem Marine Society Papers, box 1, quoted in M. V. Brewington, "The Backon on Backer's," *Essex Institute Historical Collections* 101 (1964): 50–51; Smith, "The Salem Marine Society," 275–76.

22. *Two-Hundredth Anniversary of Boston Light,* 7–8 (pamphlet in the Peabody Museum Library, Salem, Mass.). The island was named after the Elder Brewster of Plymouth.

23. Ibid., 11; Stevenson, *The World's Lighthouses before 1820,* 174–75.

24. Quotations from Benjamin Franklin's autobiography are from Stevenson, *The World's Lighthouses before 1820,* 174.

25. Francis Ross Holland, Jr., *America's Lighthouses: Their Illustrated History since 1716* (New York: Dover Publications, 1988), 10; *Two-Hundredth Anniversary of Boston Light,* 11. The cannon is exhibited today at the Coast Guard Academy in New London. Later, fog signals on Brewster's Island included a fog bell of nearly three-quarters of a ton installed in 1851, a reed trumpet using compressed air installed in 1872, and a steam siren installed in 1887.

26. *Two-Hundredth Anniversary of Boston Light,* 11.

27. In 1859, the tower was raised twenty feet and lined with brick. Ibid., 12.

28. Baker, *A History of the Boston Marine Society,* 22. Untitled newspaper clipping for 7 November 1895, in the collection of the Nantucket Historical Society.

29. Rhode Island Colonial Records, 2:6, 17 February 1730. Rhode Island State Archives.

30. Susan B. Franklin, "The Beavertail Lighthouse," *Rhode Island History* 10, no. 4 (October 1951): 98.

31. William Douglass, *A Summary . . . of the Settlements in North America,* quoted in Richard

L. Champlin, "Rhode Island's First Lighthouse," *Newport History* 43, no. 139 (Summer 1970): 49.

32. William Gilman Low, "A Short History of Beaver Tail Light, Conanicut, Rhode Island," *Bulletin of the Jamestown Historical Society* 7 (August 1936): 8–9.

33. In 1720, Dr. William Douglass was unable to find a single thermometer or barometer in Boston, and it is unlikely that any other precision instruments were readily available during these years. George H. Daniels, *Science in American Society* (New York: Alfred A. Knopf, 1971), 56.

34. Rhode Island General Assembly Acts and Resolves, June 1762, quoted in Champlin, "Rhode Island's First Lighthouse," 50; Rhode Island Colonial Records, 13:2, pp. 53ff., "Petition of Joseph Arnold," 13 February 1767, Rhode Island State Archives.

35. William Ellery to Albert Gallatin, 19 May 1804, Customs House Letter Book no. 2, quoted in Champlin, "Rhode Island's First Lighthouse," 51.

36. Caulkins, *History of New London, Connecticut* 2.

37. Ibid., 474. Robert Owen Decker, *The New London Merchants: The Rise and Decline of a Connecticut Port* (New York: Garland Publishing Co., 1986), 55–57. Stevenson, *The World's Lighthouses before 1820,* 179.

38. Stevenson, *The World's Lighthouses before 1820,* 179.

39. The Pilgrims called this peninsula "the gurnett's nose," apparently after a headland in England resembling a fish of that name caught along the coast of Devonshire (manuscript entitled, "History of Plymouth [Gurnet] Light, Massachusetts," in the collection of the Cape Ann Historical Society).

40. Baker, *A History of the Boston Marine Society,* 23–24; Stevenson, *The World's Lighthouses before 1820,* 170.

41. Caulkins, *History of New London, Connecticut,* 24.

Chapter 2: The Struggle for a System

1. *The Public Statutes at Large of the United States of America* (Boston: Charles C. Little & James Brown, 1850), 1:53–54.

2. Samuel Eliot Morison, *The Oxford History of the American People* (New York: Oxford University Press, 1965), 317.

3. "Appointments, great and small, were of direct concern to Washington, and no collector of customs, captain of a cutter, keeper of a lighthouse, or surveyor of revenue was appointed except after specific consideration by the President." Leonard D. White, *The Federalists: A Study in Administrative History* (New York: Macmillan Co. 1948), 106.

4. Benjamin Lincoln's career as a public servant began in 1757 when at age twenty-four he became town clerk of Hingham, Massachusetts. He was later a member of the Provincial Legislature and of the Provincial Congress and a brigadier general in the Revolution. He served as secretary of war from 1781 to 1783. He was lieutenant governor of Massachusetts when in 1789 he applied to Washington for a federal position, stating that he had lost much

property and that his pay as lieutenant governor was "insufficient." He served as collector of customs at Boston from 1789 until his retirement in 1809. In later years his energies were apparently somewhat reduced. He was charged by Massachusetts congressman Benjamin Goodhue with "unpardonable neglect" of Salem's Baker Island Lighthouse, and in 1798 his competency was privately questioned by Secretary of the Treasury Oliver Wolcott. White, *The Federalists*, 303–05.

5. Customs House Letter Book, Vol. 1, Newport Historical Society.

6. John Rice to Alexander Hamilton, 16 October 1789, National Archives, Lighthouse Letter Book B (New Hampshire and Massachusetts, 1789–97).

7. Wrote Benjamin Lincoln to Alexander Hamilton, "I have received a return from Knox and Houston [keeper of Cape Ann]. They accept with gratitude their appointments under the United States." 6 April 1790, National Archives, Lighthouse Letter Book B.

8. On 23 September, Lincoln submitted a bill for repairs of the lights to Hamilton, noting that the painters, unauthorized, had given them two coats. These small twin towers were an unusual solution to the common problem of shifting sand bars at a harbor entrance. The structures were mounted on sliders so that, when the bar shifted, they, too, could be moved. When a captain brought the towers into alignment, his boat could safely enter the harbor. But in practice it was not so simple. A few years later, Lincoln wrote in alarm to the commissioner of the revenue that the published sailing directions for Newburyport had become invalid: "The sands frequently shift, and thereby the directions published to the world becomes a false one which makes it necessary immediately often to change the position of the lighthouses. . . . These directions will certainly ruin the vessels on shore if attended to." Problems continued. In 1789, owners of the *Friendship* petitioned Congress for indemnification for their vessel lost at the entrance to the Merrimac River, owing to a failure to move the light to its correct position as a leading mark, after a storm. National Archives, Lighthouse Letter Book B, 6 April, 1 July 1790, 11 December 1794; George R. Putnam, *Lighthouses and Lightships of the United States* (Boston: Houghton Mifflin, 1917), 28.

9. According to Richard Boonisar of Plymouth, Massachusetts, the lease by which Thomas granted Massachusetts use of the land had specified that Thomas or his heirs would be the keepers. General Thomas had seized Dorchester Heights from the British. After the war, he went to Canada, where he contracted smallpox and died.

10. Boston Marine Society to the president of the United States, 18 November 1789, National Archives, Lighthouse Letter Book B.

11. 21 April 1795, ibid.

12. Abuses turned up as well. The keeper at Sandy Hook, wrote Tench Coxe to the collector at New York in 1793, was using far more firewood than could possibly be consumed in the stove of a lighthouse in the winter season and also more candles and soap than could be justified; but most egregious was the forty yards of cloth that he had charged to the government, "far more than needed to wipe the lantern." National Archives, micro copy 63 (roll 1), "Treasury Department Lighthouse Letters 1:65."

13. Circular sent from commissioner of the revenue, Tench Coxe, 19 July 1793, ibid. In a note to Lincoln, he added, "They are both as high as the compensations of the New York, Delaware, and Chesapeake keepers who can make very little saving of expense from fish,

and have no other opportunities of business and live upon sand hills totally unimproved. They are higher than all the rest."

14. 24 May 1794, National Archives, Lighthouse Letter Book B.

15. In 1734, the Massachusetts General Court had designated the keeper as principal pilot of the port. Sometime after Hancock's tenure ended in 1797, the pilotage was returned to the keeper. A report on the lighthouse system in 1838 criticized this practice as detrimental to the performance of the keeper's lighthouse duties. Esterquest, *State Adjustments to the Federal Constitution*, 4.

16. The boat was about fifteen tons burden, with two masts. Lincoln to Coxe, June 1796, National Archives, Lighthouse Letter Book B.

17. 2d Cong. 2d sess., Doc. 34. This listing of the salaries of all U.S. civil servants for the year ending 12 October 1792 shows that George Washington as president was paid $25,000, John Adams as vice president $5,000, and Thomas Jefferson as secretary of state and Alexander Hamilton as secretary of the Treasury each $3,500.

18. 18 July 1791, National Archives, Lighthouse Letter Book, vol. 1.

19. Tench Coxe to the secretary of the Treasury, 29 September 1795, National Archives, micro copy 63 (roll 1), "Treasury Department Lighthouse Letters 1:65." In 1828, the compensation of superintendents of lighthouses was raised to 2½ percent or a maximum of $400.

20. Tench Coxe to General Huntington, 2 August 1793, ibid.

21. *Journal*, 2d Cong., 2d sess., 1792.

22. 22 May 1794, National Archives, micro copy 63 (roll 1), "Treasury Department Lighthouse Letters 1:65."

23. "The Misery Islands," *Essex Institute Historical Collections* 38 (1902): 248. National Archives, Lighthouse Letter Book B, 30 April 1796, in which the Salem Marine Society asks representative from Salem to Congress Goodhue if the United States will purchase the soil, noting that Baker's Island is owned by a foreigner in England.

24. 30 May 1796, National Archives, Lighthouse Letter Book B.

25. Ibid., p. 25. No name or date appear on this fragment; it is probably from Lincoln to Coxe.

26. Baker, *A History of the Boston Marine Society*, 73–74. The ten acres were purchased for $100.

27. 19 April 1797, National Archives, Lighthouse Letter Book B.

28. National Archive's, Lighthouse Letter Book B, 6. September 1797, Benjamin Lincoln to Tench Coxe.

29. Lincoln to Coxe, ibid., 6 September 1797.

30. The extensive sailing directions appear in Baker, *A History of the Boston Marine Society*, 314–15.

31. Arthur R. Railton, "Gay Head Light: The Island's First," *Dukes County Intelligencer* 23, no. 3 (February 1982): 93.

32. Ibid., 94.

33. Ibid., 98, 100–101.

34. 16 November 1790, National Archives, Lighthouse Letter Book B.

35. 19 October 1791, National Archives, Lighthouse Letter Book B.

36. Letter 7 December 1819, William Ellery to Jonathan Nash. William Ellery Papers, John Hay Library, Brown University, Providence, Rhode Island.

37. In 1837, the Watch Hill light was described as "a very bad one; the lamps are bad, the reflectors too small . . . and some of them cannot be adjusted. . . . The machinery of this light is so bad that the revolutions are not regular, and it sometimes requires being turned by hand." Report of E. and G. W. Blunt, 25th Cong., 2d sess., S. Doc. 138. The report went on to say that, recently, Edmund Blunt, engaged in work for the Coast Survey, had noticed an unevenness in the lights as they revolved. He requested the keeper to remove the thick glass "lenses" before the lamps to determine if the problem was with the reflectors. "The effect was astonishing; the brilliancy was increased very much." Another observer remarked that "the light increased so much in brilliancy that they would not know what to make of it at Stonington."

38. The following is based on Arthur R. Railton's "Cape Poge Light: Remote and Lonely," *Dukes County Intelligencer* 25 (November 1983): 54–80.

39. The bill came to $1,986, $1,950 for the contractor and $36 for the land. This did not leave enough for Lincoln's commission, and the commissioner of the revenue told him to pay himself from another account. Ibid., 57–58.

40. Ibid., 60. Ebenezer Skiff, keeper of Gay Head light elsewhere on Martha's Vineyard, also had his problems. He wrote Lincoln in August 1803, "The land is very poor and is only two acres . . . but so much of it as I have manured fully answered the purposes you expected. I cannot do without the use of a horse which I am obliged to keep in a common pasture which is a considerable distance from me. . . . my firewood is costly. . . . the spring of water does not affect a sufficiency in the summer." Railton, "Gay Head Light; The Island's First," 100.

41. Railton, "Cape Poge Light," 68. Boats for lighthouses were a great need, not only for the lives the keepers might save, but for maintaining contact with towns that were often a considerable distance away. On 21 April 1795, Peleg Cotton of Nantucket wrote Coxe that the lighthouse boat for Great Point on Nantucket, the second to be supplied by the state since the light was established in 1784, needed to be replaced. Lincoln complied, but on 28 June 1796 Paul Pinkam, keeper of Great Point, wrote Coxe that, a few nights before, the boat furnished by Lincoln had been stolen from the landing point nearby. He believed that the thieves were two men who had recently broken out of jail, where they had been consigned for the robbery of the Nantucket Bank. Immediately, he wrote Coxe, he took a number of men and pursued the thieves to the mainland, but without success. He advertised in public papers for return of the boat, offering a reward of $50. National Archives, Lighthouse Letter Book B.

42. Railton, "Cape Poge Light," 64. In the same letter, Mayhew requested thirty squares of glass six by eight inches, and a diamond to cut it. "The glass I have won't fit the sashes of the Lantern."

43. The request was made by an intermediary, a customs official in Edgartown married to Mayhew's sister.

44. Railton, "Cape Poge Light," p. 75.

45. When Albert Gallatin took office as Thomas Jefferson's secretary of the Treasury, Stephen Pleasonton, then a clerk in the Treasury Department, was described to him in a note

as a "nothingarian." Henry Adams, *The Life of Albert Gallatin* (Philadelphia: J. B. Lippincott & Co., 1879), 277.

Chapter 3: The Darkest Years

1. Henry Dearborn had succeeded Benjamin Lincoln as the Boston collector on the latter's retirement in 1809. Dearborn had been a physician on Washington's staff during the Revolution, a member of Congress, and secretary of war under Jefferson. When war broke out with England in 1812, Madison placed him at the head of the northern army, and his son, Henry A. S. Dearborn, succeeded him as collector. The younger Dearborn continued in the position until 1829, when newly elected President Jackson purged the civil service and replaced him with one of his own followers.

2. Perhaps he was descended from the Rev. Mr. Lewis of Wellfleet, protagonist of a story told by Samuel Eliot Morison. One Sunday while preaching, Lewis spied through the church window a vessel running aground. Shouting "Start fair!" he descended the pulpit and led his congregation to the plunder. Morison, *The Maritime History of Massachusetts*, 149.

3. 25th Cong., 2d sess., S. Doc. 138, p. 66.

4. He equipped his consolidated operation with newly patented horse-powered ropewalk machinery, employed one hundred workers, and produced 746 tons annually. At various times, Lewis also held elective posts in city and state government. Richard Updike, "Winslow Lewis and the Lighthouses," *American Neptune* 28 (1968): 31ff. Facts about Lewis's life are also found in a memorial to his son. John H. Sheppard, *Brief Memoir of Dr. Winslow Lewis* (Cambridge, Mass.: John Wilson & Son), 1872.

5. Patent no. 891. Updike, "Winslow Lewis and the Lighthouses," 38–39.

6. Winslow Lewis, *A Review of the Report of I. W. P. Lewis* (Boston: Tuttle & Dennett, 1843), 22–23.

7. Winslow Lewis, *A Review of the Report of I. W. P. Lewis* (Boston: Tuttle & Dennett, 1843), 23–29; Baker, *A History of the Boston Marine Society*, 75–76.

8. A. Hunter Dupree, *Science in the Federal Government* (Cambridge, Mass.: Harvard University Press, 1957), 13.

9. The lack of manufacturing capability hindered invention in the early Republic. As with navigational lighting, it was the lack not so much of ideas as of a means to develop them that prolonged technological backwardness. In 1789, for instance, a forty-five-foot steam-powered vessel was developed by John Fitch, many years before Robert Fulton's success of 1807. Though backed by prominent Philadelphians, including Benjamin Franklin and William Thornton, Fitch was never able to make a salable model. Thornton later explained, "The disadvantages of never having seen a steam engine on the principles contemplated, and of not having a single engineer in our company or pay, we made engineers of common blacksmiths, and after expending many thousand dollars, the boat did not exceed three miles an hour." In debt, Fitch abandoned the enterprise and died a suicide in 1798. Oliver Evans was somewhat more successful with his version. In 1804, he demonstrated a steam-powered dredge on the Schuylkill, later writing, "Had I been patronized, as Mr. Fulton was, by the

State of New York, with the exclusive right for thirty years, and by a Mr. Livingston with thirty thousand dollars . . . I might have showed steamboats in full operation before Mr. Fulton began his boat." John Harrison Morrison, *History of American Steam Navigation* (New York: W. F. Sametz & Co., 1903), 8–11, 12–14.

10. There was no lack of models for Lewis to work from. Edmund and George Blunt believed Lewis to have copied the North Foreland light in England, privately managed at the time. Of the lenses in front of the lamp, they stated that they were immediately removed when the lighthouse came into possession of Trinity House in 1831. "The light was consequently rendered much more brilliant. There is no room for doubt, that the glasses used in our lighthouses, and which we understand are similar . . . are all injurious to the efficiency of the light. . . . It would be well worth the inquiry to ascertain the whole cost to the public of this ingenious patent to obscure the lights." U.S. Light-House Establishment, *Compilation of Public Documents . . . Relating to Lighthouses . . . 1789–1871* (Washington, D.C.: U.S. Government Printing Office, 1871), 96. D. Alan Stevenson believed that Lewis saw such lenses at the South Stack Lighthouse, first lighted February 1809. As these were 4½ inches in diameter and obstructed only 5 percent of the light rays from the 20⅝-inch parabola, they were less destructive to the light. Lewis's reflectors were 8½ inches and sixteen inches and were spherical instead of parabolic, so his lens would have obstructed 33 percent in one case and 100 percent in the other. Another lens of this sort was viewed by Robert Stevenson at Flamborough Lighthouse in December 1809. He states that the lenses were too small and thick to be useful and were soon removed from both lighthouses. Stevenson, *The World's Lighthouses before 1820*, 77, 80, 296. Lewis's nephew, I. W. P. Lewis, believed that his uncle borrowed his use of the "magnifying lens" from Holyhead Lighthouse, 27th Cong., 3d sess., H. Doc. 183, p. 51. But Winslow Lewis continued to claim originality in the face of all evidence, stating in 1838, "Whether the English took the model of their reflector from mine, I cannot say. They used reflectors in Holyhead light-house in 1810, but I do not know what their form was at that time. Those now used in England are the same as mine, but larger," 25th Cong., 2d sess., S. Doc. 138, p. 67.

11. Craig Mair, *A Star for Seamen: The Stevenson Family of Engineers* (London: Butler & Tanner, 1978), 8–14.

12. Stevenson, *The World's Lighthouses before 1820*, 54. The light was an improvement in other ways as well. The account continued, "By this construction the light is constant and certain, whereas [with the former coal-fired light] the seamen were sometimes obliged to awaken the old gentlman . . . with a shot, to put him in mind his fire wanted glowing."

13. Ibid., 16–17, 26.

14. Robert Louis Stevenson, "Thomas Stevenson, Civil Engineer" (1887), in *The Lantern Bearers and Other Essays*, ed. Jeremy Treglown (New York: Farrar, Straus, Giroux, 1988, 213).

15. A full account of the building of the Bell Rock Lighthouse is in Stevenson, *The World's Lighthouses before 1820*, 203–28. On Stevenson's innovations in lamp design, see Stevenson, pp. 94–96. His innovations included the placing of a tray below the burner to catch dripping oil, adding a frost lamp to warm the burners before lighting in cold weather, and a lamp reservoir to hold a twenty-four-hour oil supply. To improve communication with the mainland, carrier pigeons were lodged at the light to take messages ashore when needed. Four

keepers were assigned here rather than the usual two, to avoid difficulties such as had arisen at Eddystone, when one keeper had died and the other, fearing he would be accused of murder, kept the body for four weeks until the weather allowed him to bring it ashore. Mair, *A Star for Seamen*, 133.

16. Scarcity of texts and instruments, lack of funds for experimentation, and difficulties keeping abreast of European developments also hindered scientific advancement. The mathematical precosity of Nathaniel Bowditch, one of the country's first native geniuses and author of the *New American Practical Navigator*, fortunately was nourished with a library belonging to an Irish scientist captured by a Beverly privateer and housed in the Salem Philosophical Library. Morison, *The Maritime History of Massachusetts*, 114–15.

17. *The Public Statutes at Large*, 2:691.

18. "As the oil in most of the Light Houses has been gauged by me since the 1st June inst. in 1810 the annual consumption of oil in all the US Light Houses was forty-three thousand gallons, in 1811 forty-six thousand gallons, St. Simons, Cape Lookout and Scituate Light Houses having been added. None having been built since, we may state the annual consumption of the old lamps to be 46,000 gallons." The additional two thousand gallons may be what was allowed keepers for their personal use. Winslow Lewis to Henry A. S. Dearborn, 23 June 1813, National Archives, Winslow Lewis Letters, "Letters received from Lighthouse Superintendents."

19. Because of the haphazard way in which oil had been purchased and distributed up to that point, the government had to rely on the keepers' records of oil they received. When Ellery asked Nash for information on oil delivered three years before, he received the following answer: "Sorry I cannot answer fully as I did not keep a copy of the receipt I sent you in May 1809, . . . but it appears by the Bill of Laden that you shipped the 19th of April 1809 in the sloop *Mayflower* . . . for the use of the lighthouse under my care, 11 casks of winter pressed spermaceti oil from head matter, containing 569 gal. also, 11 casks of summer strained spermaceti oil containing 570 gal. . . . which you will find makes with what you have found receipts for 3182 gal." (Wm. Ellery Papers, John Hay Library, Brown University).

20. 25th Cong., 2d sess., S. Doc. 138, pp. 40, 67.

21. Lewis to Henry A. S. Dearborn, 13 August 1813, National Archives, Winslow Lewis Letters, "Letters received from Lighthouse Superintendents."

22. Henry A. S. Dearborn to Albert Gallatin, 31 August 1812, ibid.

23. Lewis to Dearborn, 13 August 1813, ibid.

24. Jonathan Nash to William Ellery, William Ellery Papers, John Hay Library, Brown University, Providence, Rhode Island.

25. Lewis to Henry A. S. Dearborn, 15 March 1815, National Archives, Winslow Lewis Letters, "Letters received from Lighthouse Superintendents."

26. Lewis to Henry A. S. Dearborn, 22 June 1813, ibid.

27. In 1810, when this new arrangement was apparently instituted, William Ellery wrote John Nash, keeper of Watch Hill, "Sir, I now send you 7 casks of winter oil marked W. (by master of sloop *Mayflower*), and 9 casks of summer oil marked S., the former to be put into the cisterns designed for winter oil, and the latter into those designed for summer oil, for which you will send me a receipt in the following form: Rec'd of Wm. E., Supt. of the Lighthouses in the district of Newport, casks of winter oil marked W. and of summer oil

marked S. and numbered as following . . . Containing in the whole 494 gal." (Wm. Ellery Papers, John Hay Library, Brown University).

28. As stated in Lewis's contract with Commissioner of the Revenue Stephen Smith. The contract also allowed keepers an annual consumption, free of charge, of up to twenty gallons of oil, instead of candles, for domestic purposes. See also 25th Cong., 2d sess., S. Doc. 138, p. 67. Richard Updike points out that in 1816 sperm oil was selling at $1.12 per gallon, allowing Lewis a profit of almost $12,500, more than twice the salary of the secretary of the Treasury and almost half that of President Madison's. He also notes that, in a letter to Pleasonton of 1817, Lewis stated that his improvements had reduced consumption of oil by 70 percent. If true, Lewis had an additional ten thousand gallons to sell or use in his cordage business.

29. Stevenson, *A Rudimentary Treatise,* 79–80.

30. A. B. Johnson, *The Modern Lighthouse Service* (Washington, D.C.: U.S. Government Printing Office, 1889), 49.

31. Winslow Lewis, *Description of the Light Houses on the Coast of the United States* (Boston: Thomas O. Bangs, 1817), 16.

32. *Essex Institute Historical Collections* 38 (1902): 249. Complaints about the change continued, and in 1820 the second tower was restored. Of different heights, the two towers were known as "Mama and Papa Baker."

33. Edmund March Blunt, *The American Coast Pilot* (Newburyport: E. M. Blunt, 1817), 144. Lewis did not change his ways. In 1835, when refitting the Mobile Point Lighthouse, he changed it from fixed to revolving without consultation. Pleasonton rebuked him for this.

34. Lewis, *Descriptions of the Light Houses,* 6. Ken Morse of the Pell Marine Science Library has kindly brought to my attention a French translation of *Descriptions,* which may be found in *Melanges sur l'Amerique,* vol. 16, class mark HT-C D16, John Carter Brown Library, Brown University. It is far more likely that the French, rather than Lewis, took on the task of translation.

35. The new contract was for five years instead of seven and allowed him one-third rather than half the oil saved, while increasing his allowance for transporting oil to $2,200 and for maintaining the apparatus to $1,500. Updike, "Winslow Lewis and the Lighthouses," 41. Pleasonton was not always easy on Lewis. When he found that Lewis claimed to have supplied oil to seventeen more lamps than the local superintendents reported, he deducted the number of gallons (thirty-nine per lamp) from Lewis's allowance and reduced it further when Lewis admitted that eight lamps that he had included on his list were not lighted.

36. 25th Cong., 2d sess., S. Doc. 428, p. 10; 25th Cong., 2d sess., S. Doc. 138, pp. 34, 67. Lewis claimed that the reason for his fall was political, resulting from the election of Andrew Jackson. In 1830 he wrote Pleasonton, stating that the government still owed him money for "bad oil" he had replaced at his own expense: "Having closed my connection with the Light House Establishment after 16 years of hard service, rather poorer in my pecuniary affairs than when I commenced, and having rather too far advanced in years to commence new pursuits," he requested that he be returned the oil that he had replaced. Updike, "Winslow Lewis and the Lighthouses," 43.

37. Lewis, *A Review of the Report of I. W. P. Lewis,* 6.

38. Naish, *Seamarks*, 116–18. *Report . . . of the Lighthouse Board* (Washington, D.C.: A. Boyd Hamilton, 1852), 69.

39. Alan Stevenson, "Sea-Lights," in *Encyclopaedia Britannica*, 7th ed. (Edinburgh: A. & C. Black, 1842), 16; Stevenson, *The World's Lighthouses before 1820*, 85; Wayne Wheeler, "Augustin Fresnel and His Magic Lantern," *Keeper's Log* 1 (Winter 1985): 8–10.

40. The first revolving light was established in 1781 by Swedish engineer Jonas Norberg at Carlsten on the west coast of Sweden. Hague and Christie, *Lighthouses*, 176.

41. *Report . . . of the Lighthouse Board*, 55.

42. Stevenson, "Sea-Lights," 28.

43. *Encyclopaedia Britannica*, 11th ed., vol. 11 (New York: Encyclopaedia Britannica Co., 1910), 209.

44. Statistics show that the Fresnel lens worked best when it mattered most. The number of shipwrecks on British coasts averaged 550 each year between 1793 and 1829, and in 1833 there were a total of eight hundred. On the shores of France, shipwrecks averaged 163 between 1816 and 1823, dropping to fifty-nine during the next eight years. Stevenson, *The World's Lighthouses before 1820*, xxiii.

45. Stevenson, "Sea-Lights," 26–27; *Report . . . of the Lighthouse Board*, 92.

46. In Massachusetts, twin lights were built at Plymouth, Cape Ann, Baker's Island, Newburyport, and Nauset; others were established at Elizabeth and Matinicus Rock in Maine and at Navesink in New Jersey. A triple light was built at Nauset in 1838, by Winslow Lewis.

47. 27th Cong., 2d sess., H. Doc. 183, pp. 46–47.

48. 27th Cong., 2d sess., H. Doc. 811, pp. 84, 18.

Chapter 4: David Melville and the Gas Lights

1. The first American David Melville had emigrated from Glascow in the late seventeenth century and married Elizabeth Willard, daughter of the Rev. Samuel Willard, vice president of Harvard College and pastor of South Church in Boston. Their son David moved to Newport in 1731. On 5 November 1742, he and his third wife, Lydia West, produced another David. He and *his* wife, Elizabeth Thurston, gave birth to their son David on 21 March 1773. Thomas Willard, another offspring of the first David Melville, was a cabinetmaker who moved to Newport around 1737 to help build the Colony House. Later, he worked on the steeple of Trinity Church, patterned after one he had previously built in Boston. This information is recorded in the Melville family Bible at the Newport Historical Society.

2. A nightclub, Pelham East, stands on the site today.

3. *Newport Mercury*, 4 June 1853.

4. A Mr. Henfry who demonstrated the gas light in Baltimore "as early as 1799 or 1800" is mentioned in Malcolm Watkins, "Artificial Lighting in America, 1830–1860," in *Annual Report of the Board of Regents of the Smithsonian Institution, 1951* (Washington, D.C.: U.S. Government Printing Office, 1952), 392, but no confirmation of this has been found elsewhere.

5. 18 March 1813, no patent number. *Newport Mercury*, 4 June 1853.

6. Six years later, a wiser Melville wrote, "The object of the writer . . . was to introduce the gas lights into the light houses as well as into manufactories, etc., while Lewis's object in forming the connexion, appears to have been to prevent the introduction of them in the light houses." David Melville, *Expose of Facts* (Providence, R.I.: Miller & Hutchins, 1819), 45.

7. He paid brassmakers Joseph Lyon and Otis Chaffee $6 for fixing the gas stove and $31.50 for making copper piping and three brass chandeliers, according to Edith May Tilley, "David Melville and His Early Experiments with Gas in Newport," *Bulletin of the Newport Historical Society*, no. 60 (January 1927): 3. In 1853, when the Newport gasworks was being built to provide gas for the city, it was Lyon and Otis who brought attention to Melville's efforts nearly forty years before.

8. *Newport Mercury*, 20, 27 February 1813, quoted in ibid., 4–6. See also the account in the *Newport Mercury*, 11 June 1853.

9. *Newport Mercury*, 11 June 1853; Tilley, "David Melville and His Early Experiments," 6.

10. Tilley, "David Melville and His Early Experiments," 6–7.

11. Letter of 15 February 1811, in George Champlin Mason, *Newport Historical and Social Reminiscences of Ye Olden Times* (1892), 4:286, Rhode Island Historical Society Library.

12. The contract is among Lighthouse Papers, box 1, National Archives Record Center, Waltham, Mass.

13. 16 April 1817 Winslow Lewis letter to William Ellery, quoted in 10 May 1817 William Ellery letter to the secretary of the Treasury, Custom House Letter Book Number 4, Newport Historical Society.

14. The lights were at Petit Manan, Tarpaulin Cove, the West Chop of Holmes Hole on Martha's Vineyard, and Nantucket. *Newport Mercury*, 17 May 1817.

15. This process, as described in the *American Gas Light Journal* of 1859, is quoted in Tilley, "David Melville and His Early Experiments," 15.

16. Letter 10 May 1817 from William Ellery, *Customs House Letter Book*, vol. 1, Newport Historical Society Library.

17. Melville stated that, to ascertain the intensity of light, the comparison of shadows was done on the principle of Count Rumford and the gas lights compared with the light of the Argand lamps as two and a half to one. In November, he noted that about ninety gallons per hour were used by each burner, producing a light equal to thirty candles of six to the pound, exclusive of the power of the reflectors.

18. The keeper's helper was Joseph Batty Carr. Nine years later, Melville recommended Carr for the position of keeper of the lighthouse to be erected at Warwick Neck, stating that Carr had lived with Captain Shearman "for seven years at the Newport light and attended David Melville's gas apparatus; and in consequence of debility is unable to obtain a livelihood by manual labor." Lighthouse Papers, box 2, National Archives Record Center, Waltham, Mass.

19. Dick Thompson, former plant supervisor for the Providence Gas Co., suggests that he used this by-product of turpentine production from Carolina pines in order to keep down costs and avoid use of imported bituminous coal.

20. David Melville, Meteorological Table and Diary, Newport Historical Society, Newport, RI, entry for 13, 14 December 1817.

21. Ibid., entry for 8, 14 January 1818.

22. Ibid., entry for 7 February 1818 and addendum.

23. Ibid., entry for 12 August 1818.

24. Letter of 10 May 1817 from Ellery, *Customs House Letter Book*, vol. 1.

25. David Melville, Meteorological Table and Diary, Newport Historical Society, Newport, RI, entry for 23 October 1817.

26. On 12 December 1853, age 80, Melville made a sworn statement regarding this discovery as "evidence of the date of a discovery and improvement for which a patent may hereafter be applyed [sic]—and to prevent any other one from surreptitiously obtaining a Patent for the same discovery and improvement."

27. William Ellery to Stephen Smith, *Customs House Letter Book* vol. 4, 10 May 1817. Newport Historical Society. Quoted in Richard Champlin, "Rhode Island's First Lighthouse," *Bulletin of the Newport Historical Society*, vol. 43, 139, part 3 (Summer 1970).

28. Ellery, *Customs House Letter Book*, no. 4, December 1817.

29. Melville later pointed out that wider use would have kept costs down considerably, Coppersmiths could have been hired at $30 per month instead of $2.50 per day plus board. Tar and rosin would have cost $1.75 wholesale rather than $2.25–$2.75 per barrel. The coal used during the first three months cost $98.65, while the wood for the remaining nine months was only $70.27 at the retail price of $4.00–$4.50 per cord. Other expenses included the cost of the building (stone, lime, lumber, labor, board of carpenters and masons, totaling $390.36) and the apparatus (which cost $971.85). Together with the fuel, costing $168.73, the grand total equaled $1,480.94.

30. *Newport Mercury*, 11 June 1853; Tilley, "David Melville and His Early Experiments," 14.

31. This handwritten account is at the Newport Historical Society. Melville begins by stating, "Nearly all my papers and letters kept during the experiment with gas at the Newport [light]house have been mislaid or lost, and I am therefore obliged to write what I can in relation to its termination from the best of my recollection, after a lapse of thirty-six years, and in the eight-second year of my age." A letter dated 20 November 1818 from the commissioner of the revenue denies Melville continuation of his experiment. Lighthouse Papers, box 1, National Archives Record Center, Waltham, Mass.

32. Melville, *An Expose of Facts*, 6.

33. The device worked by means of a copper funnel positioned over the flame and a wire from this transmitting heat through oil in the fountain of the lamp.

34. "At this moment, as if he viewed me with an eye of intuition, he stopped me, and observed, that we had been so long friends it would be a pity we should get at variance about a thing which was not of so much consequence as I appeared to attach to it." Lewis proposed to Melville that they "make the best bargain we could with the government to introduce the improvement into the Light Houses, and make it a joint concern." Melville declined, stating that he would rather sell out his right to him. Lewis replied that he hoped they might agree on terms later. Melville, *Expose of Facts*, 16–17.

35. Melville gave bonds for $10,000 "for the security of the light house against fire."

36. The specifications for the warming lamp are in Melville, *Expose of Facts*, 4.

37. Melville, *Expose of Facts*, 7, 47; and Light House Papers, box 1, leter dated 24 October 1818, National Archives Record Center, Waltham, Mass., In *Expose of Facts*, 47, Melville notes that soon after Lewis "contracted with Zenas Coffin of Nantucket for a large quantity of oil . . . whether in this contract he has turned the alarm created there by the experiment with gas, to his advantage, we are left to conjecture."

38. "The improvement consists in having a tight scuttle door to close at pleasure the communication with the lantern from the bay next below; and the lantern fitted with four or more air ports . . . so as to be closed at pleasure." Melville, *Expose of Facts*, 10. Lewis replied to his claim of originality, "I have lately tried an Experiment which had the [same] effect but it is expensive, I Double Glaised the lantern leaving a space between the panes of ⅜ inch, making both tight, as no cold can pass through confined air."

39. This was not the only patent challenge in which Lewis was involved. In 1817, Francis Lowell, director of the Patent Pump Co., formed to develop the triangular valve pump invented in 1813 by Jacob Perkins, brought similar action against Lewis. Lewis owned a somewhat similar pump patented by a James Baker in 1817. The jury concluded that the two were substantially different and decided in favor of Lewis. Greville Bathe and Dorothy Bathe, *Jacob Perkins: His Inventions, His Times, and His Contemporaries* (Philadelphia: Historical Society of Pennsylvania, 1943), 54, 178–81.

40. U.S. Lighthouse Establishment. Compilation of Public Documents and Extracts from Reports and Papers relating to Lighthouses, Light Vessels, and Illuminating Apparatus, and to Beacons, Buoys and Fog Signals, 1789 to 1871. Washington: Government Printing Office, 1871, 207.

41. His contract for Dutch Island stated that he would provide it with eight patent lamps (with heaters) plus reflectors, two spare lamps, five tin butts of ninety gallons each for oil, "and all the necessary apparatus in the same manner as Light Houses in the United States are usually fitted." For this work he was paid $260. The Dutch Island Lighthouse was built by Westgate Watson and William Hollaway of North Kingstown and the Warwick Neck lighthouse by Charles Whitfield. The contracts are in the Lighthouse Papers, box 3, National Archives New England Region, Waltham, Mass.

42. Documents relating to repair of Beavertail in the Lighthouse Papers, box 3, National Archives New England Region, Waltham, Mass. The previous lantern may have been that installed in 1808 by Abisha Woodward, a New London housewright noted for his work on the New London Lighthouse. At Beavertail, Woodward raised the tower sixteen feet, added a window, floor, and flight of stairs, and constructed an iron lantern with a complete set of copper lamps and a lightning rod. For raising the tower, he was granted permission by nearby property owners Taber and Clark to "take from the rocks on their shore which are the state's as many stones as he pleases—but the loose stones on the shore will be wanted on their farm. Mr. Clarke says that the rocks being of the state can be easily split with an iron bar." Items at the John Hay Library, Brown University.

43. *Newport Mercury*, 11 June 1853.

44. Stevenson, *The World's Lighthouses before 1820*, 278.

45. 28th Cong., 2d, sess., S. Doc. 166, p. 15. Trinity House later rejected gas for light-

houses in England, citing the difficulty of delivering materials to remote sites and concern about entrusting operations to untrained keepers.

46. *Report . . . of the Light House Board*, 273–74. In 1838, Pleasonton claimed to have engaged a man some years previously who had "supplied the principal hotels and other public houses in Baltimore with gaslight, to fit up the light-house at Point Lookout, at the mouth of the Potomac." Having done so, he reported that the expense would be about equal to that of oil but that the apparatus would be so liable to get out of order that he did not advise it. 25th Cong., 2d sess., S. Doc. 138, p. 33.

47. Ibid., 151. Gas never did come into wide use for lighthouses. A. B. Johnson, writing in 1889, noted a few instances where compressed gas was used but commented, "Though the action of the illuminant is not unsatisfactory, it can hardly be said that it has yet passed beyond the point where there is not something more desired." Johnson, *The Modern Lighthouse Service*, 57. D. Alan Stevenson, noting a few early European uses of gas as a fuel for lighthouses, noted that, in more recent times, illuminants of greater intensity were provided more easily. Stevenson, *The World's Lighthouses before 1820*, 278–79.

48. Elmo Paul Hohman. *American Whaleman: A Study of Life and Labor in the Whaling Industry* (New York: Longmans, Green & Co., 1928), 4–5, 273. According to Walter S. Tower, *A History of the American Whale Fishery* (Philadelphia: University of Pennsylvania, 1901), 51, in 1846 all investments connected with the business had a value of at least $70,000,000, and it was the chief support of seventy thousand persons.

49. From an editorial of 29 June 1852 in the *Whaleman's Shipping List and Merchants' Transcript*, quoted in Judith A. Boss and Joseph D. Thomas, *New Bedford: A Pictorial History* (Norfolk, Va.: Donning Publishing Co., 1983), 63. Thanks to Dick Thompson for bringing this to my attention.

Chapter 5: Reform

1. John F. Campbell, *History and Bibliography of the New American Practical Navigator and the American Coast Pilot* (Salem, Mass.: Peabody Museum, 1964), 37, 34, 37.

2. 25th Cong., 2d sess., S. Doc. 138, pp. 6, 34.

3. The vessel was the *America*, which wrecked at the Tortugas, Florida. 25th Cong., 2d sess., S. Doc. 258, p. 8.

4. 25th Cong., 2d sess., S. Doc. 159, pp. 3, 5.

5. Ibid., 2–3.

6. Ibid 33ff.; Charles G. Maytum, *Outline of Hog Island* (1977, typescript), 38–44.

7. 25th Cong., 2d sess., H. Doc. 41, p. 4.

8. 25th Cong., 2d sess., S. Doc. 428; 27th Cong., 3d sess., H. Doc. 183, p. 52.

9. 25th Cong., 2d sess., S. Doc. 258, pp. 38–39.

10. 26th Cong., 1st sess., S. Doc. 619, pp. 3–4.

11. Ibid., 4, 7.

12. Ibid., 12. Thomas Stevenson, engineer of Scotland's Commission of the Northern

Lights, had his own view of Perry's visit. He wrote in a letter to his son dated 21 September 1838, "You have perhaps heard that the United States sent over Captain Perry of their Navy to see our European lighthouses and directed his attention especially to the Scottish lights. He had letters to me and David, but like too many, he arrived pressed for time. He went to Inchkrith with Swan [Stevenson's son-in-law], for we were all from home; they spent an hour there and the evening at the Waterloo; and off he set for Paris. . . . What in the name of wonder do people make journeys for crying all the while to themselves, haste, haste. . . . A sea captain will not make a good engineer. They should have sent a mechanical philosopher, or in other words a civil engineer." *The Manuscripts of Robert Louis Stevenson: Records of a Family of Engineers*, ed. J. Christian Bay (Chicago: Walter M. Hill, 1929), 74.

13. Wrote Perry, "Monsieur Fresnel . . . feeling a deep interest in the perfection of the machines ordered by the American government, generously undertook to superintend their construction . . . ; and I am informed by him that they will possess several valuable improvements, and be superior to any that have ever been made by the well-known manufacturere Monsieur Lepaute." 26th Cong., 1st sess., S. Doc. 619, p. 5.

14. 26th Cong., 2d sess., S. Doc. 35, pp. 2–3.

15. *Report . . . of the Light House Board*, 21–22. Of the fifteen reflector lights that Perry brought from England, fourteen were installed in the Boston lighthouse by I. W. P. Lewis, Winslow's nephew, and the other left with Pleasonton. The original intention had been to compare this reflector with Lewis's model and another built by the Blunts, but, when arrival of the reflectors was also delayed, the experiment was not carried out. In 1851, the Light House Board inspected the reflector apparatus in the Boston light, finding that it was "much worn, and has not had the care and attention it deserved." Ibid., 44.

16. I. W. P. Lewis's aptitude for mechanical construction may have been influenced by his maternal grandfather, Lemuel Cox, one of the country's few skilled engineers in the years after the Revolution. Cox's greatest triumph was the construction in 1786 of a deep-water bridge between Boston and Charleston, the first to link the city with the mainland, at what was considered an impossible site. He also built bridges at Malden and Salem. F. W. D. Holbrook and Joseph Willard, "Memoir of Isaiah William Penn Lewis," in *Biographical Archive of American Civil Engineers*, 1897, 23:428, Smithsonian Institution.

17. For his trouble, Lewis received $150 for six months' work plus travel expenses, and nothing for living expenses. 27th Cong., 3d sess., H. Doc. 183, p. 6. For Winslow Lewis's version of these incidents, see Lewis, *A Review of the Report of I. W. P. Lewis*, 53–54.

18. The actual construction of the Saybrook Lighthouse was performed by John Bishop of New London. 27th Cong., 2d sess., H. Doc. 183, p. 9.

19. Ibid., 52.

20. 27th Cong., 2d sess., H. Doc. 811, pp. 18, 84, 96.

21. 27th Cong., 3d sess., H. Doc. 183, pp. 19–20.

22. Ibid., 58.

23. Arthur R. Railton, "Cape Poge Light: Remote and Lonely, Pt. 2," *Dukes County Intelligencer* 25 (February 1984): 94.

24. The keepers' retractions are printed in Lewis, *A Review of the Report of I. W. P. Lewis*, 36–51.

25. Johnson, *The Modern Light House Service*, 19.

26. Ibid., 18.

27. 29th Cong., 1st sess., H. Doc. 222. *The Modern Light House Service*, Johnson, 19–20.

28. Stephen Pleasonton, *List of Light-Houses, Beacons, and Floating Lights of the United States* (Washington D.C.: Gideon & Co., 1849).

29. 31st Cong., 2d sess., H. Doc. 14, p. 3.

30. Harold L. Burstyn, *At the Sign of the Quadrant; An Account of the Contributions to American Hydrography Made by Edmund March Blunt and His Sons* (Mystic, CT: Marine Historical Association, 1957), 49–50.

31. *Report . . . of the Light House Board*, 35, 119–21, 154–55, 25–26, 78–79.

32. In 1848, the report noted, thirteen lighthouses in Massachusetts and eight in Maine required extensive repair.

33. Ibid., 106–7, 125, 49, 125–26, 67–68. The report noted that, although Pleasonton issued a circular directing the collectors to report all changes in lights, beacons, and buoys to the superintendent of the Coast Survey so that they might be placed on charts, "*but one collector ever complied with the direction.*"

34. Ibid., 62.

35. Ibid., 123–24.

36. Ibid., 148.

37. Ibid., 152–53.

38. Railton, "Cape Poge Light," 101–2.

39. Campbell, *History and Bibliography of the New American Practical Navigator and the American Coast Pilot*, 40.

40. Holland, *America's Lighthouses*, 36ff. "The History of the Administration of the USLH Service," *Keeper's Log* 5, no. 3 (Spring 1989): 12.

Chapter 6: Keepers and Their Families

1. Arthur R. Railton, "Gay Head Light Gets the Wondrous Fresnel," *Dukes County Intelligencer*, 23, no. 4 (May 1982): 147–48.

2. Report of 1 August 1850 by Edward W. Lawton, collector of customs for Newport, in Light House Letter Book and Records, 1844–53, Newport Historical Society.

3. 23 September 1845. William P. Babcock to B. J. Walker, secretary of the Treasury.

4. 11 May 1845. Cyrus Champlin to President-elect James K. Polk.

5. 7 August 1845. Christopher A. Sweet to the secretary of the Treasury.

6. April 1845. A. F. Potter, to the President.

7. 27 Cong., 3d sess., H. Doc. 183, pp. 163–64.

8. Johnson, *The Modern Light House Service*, 102–3.

9. Ibid., 103.

10. Ibid., 103–4.

11. Sue Ellen Thompson, "The Light Is My Child," *Log of Mystic Seaport* 32, no. 3 (Fall 1980): 92.

Catalog of Lights

1. *Keeper's Log* 2, no. 2 (Winter 1986: 27; and 3, no. 2 (Winter 1987): 26–27.

2. Elinor De Wire, "Return of Cape Cod's Three Sisters," *Keeper's Log* 3, no. 4 (Summer 1987): 24–25.

3. Holland, *America's Lighthouses*, 77–78.

4. Special thanks to Don Davidson for this information.

5. Robert M. Downie, *Block Island Lighthouses* (Block Island, R.I.: Block Island Historical Society, 1985).

6. Robert G. Bachand, *Northeast Lights; Lighthouses and Lightships, Rhode Island to Cape May, New Jersey*, pp. 32–34 (Norwalk, Conn.: Sea Sports Publications, 1989).

7. Ibid., 49–50.

8. *Historic Sites Survey, Inventory, and Analysis of Aids to Navigation in the State of Connecticut* (West Chester, Pa.: John Milner Associates, 1986), 19–22. Joel E. Helander, *The Island Called Faulkner's* (Guilford, Conn.: Joel E. Helander 1988).

9. *Historic Sites Survey*, 22–26.

10. Bachand, *Northeast Lights*, 92–94.

11. *Historic Sites Survey*, 34–38.

12. Ibid., 38–40.

13. Ibid., 40–43.

14. Ibid., 44–47.

15. Ibid., 47–50.

Bibliography

Adams, Henry. *The Life of Albert Gallatin.* Philadelphia: J. B. Lippincott & Co., 1879.

Adams, W. H. Davenport. *Lighthouses and Lightships: A Descriptive and Historical Account of Their Mode of Construction and Organization.* New York: Charles Scribner & Co., 1870.

Allen, William. *Accounts of Shipwreck and of Other Disasters at Sea, Designed to Be Interesting and Useful to Mariners, with an Appendix, Containing Dr. Payson's Address to Seamen, and a Few Prayers for Their Use.* Compiled by a Friend of Seamen. Brunswick, Maine: Printed by Joseph Griffin, 1823.

American Guide Series. *Boston Looks Seaward: The Story of the Port, 1630–1940.* Compiled by Workers of the Writers' Program of the Work Projects Administration in the State of Massachusetts. Boston: Bruce Humphries, 1941.

Annual Report of the Operations of the United States Life-saving Service. Washington, D.C.: U.S. Government Printing Office, 1876.

Baker, William A. *A History of the Boston Marine Society, 1742–1967.* Boston: Boston Marine Society, 1968.

Bathe, Greville, and Dorothy Bathe. *Jacob Perkins: His Inventions, His Times, and His Contemporaries.* Philadelphia: Historical Society of Pennsylvania, 1943.

Bay, J. Christian, ed. *The Manuscripts of Robert Louis Stevenson: Records of a Family of Engineers.* Chicago: Walter M. Hill, 1929.

Bedini, Silvio A. *Thinkers and Tinkers: Early American Men of Science.* New York: Charles Scribner's Sons, 1975.

Blunt, Edmund March. *The American Coast Pilot.* Newburyport, Mass.: Edmund M. Blunt, various years.

Blunt, E., and G. W. Blunt. *The American Coast Pilot.* New York: Edmund and George W. Blunt, various years.

Boss, Judith A., and Joseph D. Thomas. *New Bedford: A Pictorial History*, Norfolk, Va.: Donning Publishing Co., 1983.

Bowditch, Harold. *Nathaniel Bowditch.* Salem, Mass: Peabody Museum, 1937.

Brewington, M. V. "The Backon on Backer's." *Essex Institute Historical Collections* (Salem, Mass.) 101, no. 1 (January 1965): 50–55.

Bridenbaugh, Carl. *The Colonial Craftsman.* New York: New York University Press, 1950.

———. *Peter Harrison, American Architect.* Chapel Hill: University of North Carolina Press, 1949.

Bridgewater, William, and Elizabeth J. Sherwood, eds. *The Columbia Encyclopedia.* New York: Columbia University Press, 1956.

Bruce, Robert V. *The Launching of Modern American Science, 1846–1876.* New York: Alfred A. Knopf, 1987.

Burstyn, Harold L. *At the Sign of the Quadrant: An Account of the Contributions to American Hydrography Made by Edmund March Blunt and His Sons.* Mystic, Conn.: Marine Historical Association, 1957.

Butler, Francis H. and Silvanus Phillips Thompson. "Compass." In *Encyclopaedia Britannica,* 11th ed. New York: Encyclopaedia Britannica Co., 1910.

Calder, Jenni. *RLS: A Life Study.* London: Hamish Hamilton, 1980.

Campbell, John F. *History and Bibliography of the New American Practical Navigator and the American Coast Pilot,* Salem, Mass.: Peabody Museum, 1964.

Caulkins, Frances Manwaring. *History of New London, Connecticut, from the First Survey of the Coast in 1612, to 1852.* New London, Conn., 1852.

Champlin, Richard L. "Rhode Island's First Lighthouse." *Newport History* 43, no. 139 (Summer 1970): 49–64.

Committee on History and Heritage of American Civil Engineering. *The Civil Engineer: His Origins.* Historical Publication no. 1. New York: American Society of Civil Engineers, 1970.

Coulson, Thomas. "The Story of Aids to Navigation." *Journal of the Franklin Institute* 248, no. 4 (October 1949): 273–304.

Daniels, George H. *Science in American Society.* New York: Alfred A. Knopf, 1971.

Decker, Robert Owen. *The New London Merchants: The Rise and Decline of a Connecticut Port.* New York: Garland Publishing Co., 1986.

Dupree, A. Hunter. *Science in the Federal Government.* Cambridge, Mass.: Harvard University Press, 1957.

Emerson, Amelia Forbes. *Early History of Naushon Island.* 1935. 2d ed., Boston: Howland & Co., 1981.

Engel, Norma. *Three Beams of Light.* San Diego: Tecolote Publications, 1986.

Esterquest, Frank L. *State Adjustments to the Federal Constitution, 1789–1800.* Chicago: University of Chicago Press, 1943.

Field, Edward. *Revolutionary Defences in Rhode Island.* Providence, R.I.: Preston & Rounds, 1896.

Franklin, Benjamin. "Maritime Observations" ["A Letter from Dr. Benjamin Franklin to Mr. Alphonsus le Roy, . . . Containing Sundry Maritime Observations," August 1785]. In *The Writings of Benjamin Franklin,* vol. 9, ed. Albert Henry Smyth. New York: Macmillan Co., 1906.

Franklin, Susan B. "The Beavertail Lighthouse." *Rhode Island History* 10, no. 4 (October 1951): 97–101.

Fraser, Robert. "Scituate Lighthouse." *Keeper's Log* 3, no. 2 (Winter 1987): 2–7.

Gardner, Arthur H., comp. *A List of the Wrecks around Nantucket since the Settlement of the Island and the Incidents Connected Therewith, Embracing over 500 Vessels.* Nantucket, Mass., 1877.

Goode, G. Brown. "The Origins of the National Scientific and Educational Institutions of the United States." In *Papers of the American Historical Association*, vol. 4. New York: G. P. Putnam's Sons, 1890.

Hague, Douglas B., and Rosemary Christie. *Lighthouses: Their Architecture, History and Archeology*. Llandysul Dyfed, Wales: Gomer Press, 1975.

Heap, Major D. P. *Ancient and Modern Light-Houses*. Boston: Ticknor & Co., 1889.

Hindle, Brooke. *The Pursuit of Science in Revolutionary America*. New York: W. W. Norton & Co., 1956.

Hohman, Elmo Paul. *American Whaleman: A Study of Life and Labor in the Whaling Industry*. New York: Longmans, Green & Co., 1928.

Holbrook. F.W.D., and Joseph Willard. "Memoir of Isaiah William Penn Lewis." In *Biographical Archive of American Civil Engineers*, vol. 23. 1897. Washington, D.C., Smithsonian Institution, Division of Mechanical and Civil Engineering, National Museum of American History.

Holland, Francis Ross, Jr. *America's Lighthouses: Their Illustrated History since 1716*. New York: Dover Publications, 1988.

Jenkins, Lawrence Waters. "Marine Society at Salem in New England: A Brief Sketch of Its History." *Essex Institute Historical Collections* (Salem, Mass.) 76, no. 3 (July 1940): 199–220.

Johnson, A. B. *The Modern Lighthouse Service*. Washington, D.C.: U.S. Government Printing Office, 1889.

Lewis, Winslow. *Description of the Light Houses on the Coast of the United States*. Boston: Thomas O. Bangs, 1817.

————. *A Review of the Report of I. W. P. Lewis, on The State of the Lighthouses on the Coasts of Maine and Massachusetts*. Boston: Tuttle & Dennett, 1843.

Low, William Gilman. "A Short History of the Beaver Tail Light, Conanicut, Rhode Island." *Bulletin of the Jamestown Historical Society* 7 (August 1936).

Lunge, Georg, "Gas." In *Encyclopaedia Britannica*, 11th ed. New York: Encyclopaedia Britannica Co., 1910.

Mair, Craig. *A Star for Seamen: The Stevenson Family of Engineers*. London: Butler & Tanner, 1978.

Mason, George Champlin. *Newport Historical and Social Reminiscences*, vol. 4. Providence, R.I., Rhode Island Historical Society Library. Scrapbook.

Maytum, Charles Gregory. "Outline of Hog Island." 1973. Typescript.

Melville, David. *Expose of Facts*. Providence: Miller & Hutchins, 1819.

————. "Meteorological Table and Diary." 1817–1818. Newport, R.I., Newport Historical Society. MS.

"The Misery Islands, and What Has Happened There." *Essex Institute Historical Collections* (Salem, Mass.) 38, no. 3 (July 1902): 225–56.

Morfill, William Richard. "Navigation." *Encyclopaedia Britannica*, 11th ed. New York: Encyclopaedia Britannica Co., 1910.

Morison, Samuel Eliot. *The Maritime History of Massachusetts, 1783–1860*. Boston: Houghton Mifflin, 1961.

————. *The Oxford History of the American People*. New York: Oxford University Press, 1965.

Morrison, John Harrison. *History of American Steam Navigation*. New York: W. F. Sametz & Co., 1903.

Naish, John. *Seamarks: Their History and Development*. London: Stanford Maritime, 1985.

Nemetz, Gail. "Lore Connected with Lighthouses along the New England Coastline." 1974. Typescript.

Parsons, Eleanor C. *Thachers, Island of the Twin Lights*. Canaan, N.H.: Phoenix Publishing, 1985.

Peabody Museum of Salem. *The Marine Room of the Peabody Museum of Salem*. Salem, Mass.: Peabody Museum, 1921.

Pleasonton, Stephen. *List of Light-Houses, Beacons, and Floating Lights of the United States, in Operation on the 1st of July, 1848*. Washington, D.C.: Gideon & Co., 1849.

Preuss, Anne M., and Donald L. Treworgy. "Taking a Departure: The Navigational Instruments and Artistry of Captain Charles Harvey Townshend." *Log of Mystic Seaport* 39, no. 1 (Spring 1987): 21–34.

Public Statutes at Large of the United States of America, vol. 1. Boston: Charles C. Little & James Brown, 1850.

Putnam, George R. *Lighthouses and Lightships of the United States*. Boston: Houghton Mifflin, 1917.

————. *Sentinel of the Coasts: The Log of a Lighthouse Engineer*. New York: W. W. Norton & Co., 1937.

Railton, Arthur R. "Cape Poge Light: Remote and Lonely." *Dukes County Intelligencer* 25, no. 2 (November 1983): 54–80; 25, no. 3 (February 1984): 91–123.

————. "Gay Head Light Gets the Wonderful Fresnel." *Dukes County Intelligencer* 23, no. 4 (May 1982): 139–71.

————. "Gay Head Light: The Island's First. *Dukes County Intelligencer*. 23, no. 3 (February 1982): 91–116.

Report of the Officers Constituting the Light-House Board, Convened under Instructions from the Secretary of the Treasury, to Inquire into the Condition of the Light-House Establishment of the United States, under the Act of March 3, 1851. Washington, D.C.: A. Boyd Hamilton, 1852.

Reynaud, Francois Leonce. *Memoir upon the Light-House Illumination of the Coasts of France*. Washington, D.C.: Government Printing Office, 1871.

Rutherford, Don. "Cordouan Lighthouse Fit for a King." *Keeper's Log* 1, no. 2 (Winter 1985): 15–17.

Smith, Philip C. F. "The Salem Marine Society, 1766–1966." *American Neptune* 26 (1966): 272–79.

Starbuck, Alexander. *History of the American Whale Fishery from Its Earliest Inception to the Year 1876*. New York: Argosy-Antiquarian, 1964.

Stevenson, Alan. *Account of the Skerryvore Lighthouse, with Notes on the Illumination of Lighthouses*. London: Longman & Co., 1848

————. *A Rudimentary Treatise on the History, Construction, and Illumination of Lighthouses*, London: John Weale, 1850.

————. "Sea-Lights." In *Encyclopaedia Britannica*, 7th ed. Edinburgh: A. & C. Black, 1842.

Stevenson, D. Alan. *The World's Lighthouses before 1820*. London: Oxford University Press, 1959.

Stevenson, Robert Louis. *The Lantern Bearers and Other Essays*. Edited by Jeremy Treglown. New York: Farrar, Straus, Giroux, 1988.

Talbot, Frederick A. *Lightships and Lighthouses*. Philadelphia: J. B. Lippincott Co., 1913.

Thompson, Sue Ellen. "The Light Is My Child." *Log of Mystic Seaport* 32, no. 3 (Fall 1980): 90–98.

Tower, Walter S. *A History of the American Whale Fishery*. Political Economy and Public Law, no. 20. Philadelphia: University of Pennsylvania, 1907.

Updike, Richard W. "Winslow Lewis and the Lighthouses." *American Neptune* 28 (1968): 31–48.

U.S. Congress. House. 25th Cong. 2d.sess. H. Doc. 41.

———. 27th Cong. 3d sess. H. Doc. 183.

———. 27th Cong. 2d sess. H. Doc. 811.

———. 31st Cong. 2d sess. H. Doc. 14.

U.S. Congress. Senate. 25th Cong. 2d sess. S. Doc. 159.

———. 25th Cong. 2d sess. S. Doc. 258.

———. 25th Cong. 2d sess. S. Doc. 428.

———. 26th Cong. 1st sess. S. Doc. 619.

———. 26th Cong. 2d sess. S. Doc. 35.

U.S. Light-House Establishment. *Compilation of Public Documents and Extracts from Reports and Papers Relating to Lighthouses . . . 1789 to 1871*. Washington, D.C.: U.S. Government Printing Office, 1871.

Waters, David. *The Art of Navigation in Elizabethan and Early Stuart Times*. New Haven, Conn.: Yale University Press, 1958.

———. Elizabethan Navigation." In *Sir Francis Drake and the Famous Voyage, 1577–1580*, ed. Norman J. W. Thrower. Berkeley: University of California Press, 1984.

Watkins, C. Malcolm. *Artificial Lighting in America, 1830–1860*." 1951 Annual Report of the Board of Regents of the Smithsonian Institution. Washington, D.C.: U.S. Government Printing Office, 1952.

Watson, W. L. "History of Jamestown." *Rhode Island Historical Society Collections* 20, no. 3 (July 1929).

Wheeler, Wayne. "Augustin Fresnel and His Magic Lantern." *Keeper's Log*. 1, no. 2 (Winter 1985): 8–10.

———. "The Eddystone." Parts I–IV. *Keeper's Log* 1, no. 4 (Summer 1985):14–19; 2, no. 1 (Fall 1985): 14–18; 2, no. 2 (Winter 1986): 15–21; 2, no. 3 (Spring 1986): 23–26.

White, Leonard D. *The Federalists: A Study in Administrative History*. New York: Macmillan Co., 1948.

Whitehill, Walter Muir. *The East India Marine Society and the Peabody Museum of Salem: A Sesquicentennial History*. Salem, Mass.: Peabody Museum, 1949.

Willoughby, Malcolm F. *Lighthouses of New England*. Boston: T. O. Metcalf Co., 1929.

Wroth, Lawrence C. *The Way of a Ship: An Essay on the Literature of Navigational Science*. Portland, Maine: Southworth-Anthoensen Press, 1937.

1. Great Captain Island, Greenwich
2. Chatham Ledge, Stamford
3. Sheffield Island, Norwalk
4. Greens Ledge, Norwalk
5. Peck Ledge, Norwalk
6. Penfield Reef, Fairfield
7. Fayerweather Island, Bridgeport
8. Tongue Point, Bridgeport
9. Stratford Shoal, Stratford
10. Stratford Point, Stratford
11. New Haven Harbor, New Haven
12. Southwest Ledge, New Haven
13. Faulkner's Island, Guilford
14. Saybrook Breakwater, Old Saybrook
15. Lynde Point, Old Saybrook
16. New London Harbor, New London
17. New London Ledge, New London
18. Morgan Point, Noank
19. Latimer Reef, Stonington
20. Stonington Harbor, Stonington
21. Watch Hill, Westerly
22. Point Judith, Narragansett
23. Whale Rock, Narragansett
24. Beavertail, Jamestown
25. Dutch Island, Jamestown
26. Plum Beach, North Kingstown
27. Conanicut North, Jamestown
28. Poplar Point, Wickford
29. Wickford Harbor, Wickford
30. Warwick, Warwick
31. Conimicut, Warwick
32. Pomham Rock, East Providence
33. Sabin Point, East Providence

34. Bullock's Point, East Providence
35. Nayatt Point, Barrington
36. Bristol Ferry, Bristol
37. Hog Island Shoal, Portsmouth
38. Musselbed Shoal, Portsmouth
39. Sandy Point, Prudence Island
40. Gould Island, Portsmouth
41. Gull Rocks, Newport
42. Rose Island, Newport
43. Goat Island, Newport
44. Lime Rock, Newport
45. Castle Hill, Newport
46. North, Block Island
47. Southeast, Block Island
48. Sakonnet, Little Compton
49. Borden Flats, Fall River
50. Clark's Point, New Bedford
51. Butler Flats, New Bedford
52. Palmer Island, New Bedford
53. Cuttyhunk, Cuttyhunk Island
54. Ned Point, Mattapoisett
55. Bird Island, Marion
56. Cleveland Ledge, Bourne
57. Wing's Neck, Bourne
58. Tarpaulin Cove, Naushon Island
59. Nobska Point, Falmouth
60. Gay Head, Martha's Vineyard
61. West Chop, Martha's Vineyard
62. East Chop, Martha's Vineyard
63. Edgartown, Martha's Vineyard
64. Cape Poge, Martha's Vineyard
65. Brant Point, Nantucket
66. Great Point, Nantucket

67. Sankaty Head, Nantucket
68. Hyannis, Hyannis
69. Point Gammon, West Yarmouth
70. Bass River, West Dennis
71. Stage Harbor, Chatham
72. Monomoy, Chatham
73. Chatham, Chatham
74. Nauset Beach, North Eastham
75. Highland, Truro
76. Race Point, Provincetown
77. Wood End, Provincetown
78. Long Point, Provincetown
79. Sandy Neck, Barnstable
80. Plymouth, Plymouth
81. Duxbury Pier, Duxbury
82. Scituate, Scituate
83. Minot's Ledge, Cohasset
84. Boston, Boston
85. Long Island Head, Boston
86. Deer Island, Winthrop
87. The Graves, Boston
88. Marblehead, Marblehead
89. Derby Wharf, Salem
90. Fort Pickering, Salem
91. Baker's Island, Salem
92. Hospital Point, Beverly
93. Eastern Point, Gloucester
94. Ten Pound Island, Gloucester
95. Cape Ann (Thacher's Island), Rockport
96. Straitsmouth Island, Rockport
97. Annisquam Harbor, Annisquam
98. Newburyport Harbor, Newburyport

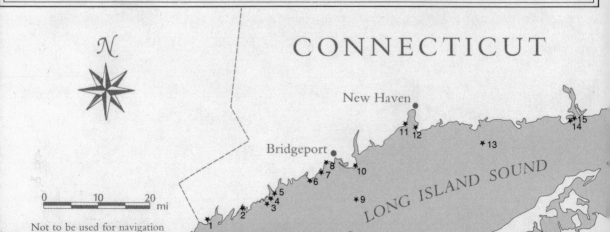

CONNECTICUT

New Haven

Bridgeport

LONG ISLAND SOUND

0   10   20
mi

Not to be used for navigation